Anna Lowell Woodbury

Lessons in cookery

Anna Lowell Woodbury

Lessons in cookery

ISBN/EAN: 9783744785860

Printed in Europe, USA, Canada, Australia, Japan

Cover: Foto ©Lupo / pixelio.de

More available books at **www.hansebooks.com**

MANUALS OF DOMESTIC WORK.
NO. 1.

Lessons in Cookery,

PREPARED FOR THE

First Mission School of Cookery and Housework.

AND FOR USE IN THE

PUBLIC SCHOOLS.

BY

Mrs. Anna Lowell Woodbury.

WASHINGTON:
ROBT. S. COOPER, PRINTER.
1889.

Entered according to act of Congress, in the year 1889, by
MRS. ANNA LOWELL WOODRUFF *Bury*
In the office of the Librarian of Congress, at Washington.

PREFACE.

There is nothing in these lessons which will be new to any experienced housekeeper; for I have merely tried to arrange as clearly and concisely as possible some of the more important facts and principles of practical cookery, in such a form as would best impress them upon the minds of the pupils. If these are fixed in their memories while they are young, they will never be entirely forgotten, even if not put immediately into practice.

The lessons were planned and partially written about ten years ago, when the school was first established, and were afterwards completed, and carefully arranged for use in the public schools; where the classes follow each other in rapid succession, and it is important that as much information as possible should be given in a limited time. They have been in daily use in the mission school for five years, and I have myself closely observed each lesson as it was given to class after class; and have made any little additions or changes which were needed. Families and individuals differ so much in their tastes, and their methods of living, that it would be impossible, in any school of cookery, to please every one; but a good foundation can be laid, and if the facts and principles of practical cookery are well understood it is very easy to vary the preparation of any particular dish. The first nineteen lessons are intended to teach the various processes of cooking, and such dishes were selected to exemplify them as would be attractive and interesting to the pupils, and useful to them in their homes. For several of the recipes I am indebted to friends, and the others were obtained from experienced practical cooks; they have, however, all been more or less changed, and in most of them very little is left as it was originally given to me. There are many others which are equally good, but these have been thoroughly tested by the young ladies who have had charge of the classes, and by hundreds of girls, and they have proved very satisfactory and well adapted to the purpose they are intended to serve. I saw that it was impossible to have system or method in schools of cookery, without a text-book; and that no teacher could give her attention to the proper preparation of the dishes, and at the same time remember to tell her pupils the many little facts which it was so important they should know. If the lessons are dictated, each pupil should bring a tablet and pencil to the class, and should copy the lesson again at home neatly in a book, with pen and ink; and these books ought to be brought in every month to the teacher, to be examined and corrected. If not dictated, they should be studied and recited like any other lessons, and the pupils should be frequently questioned in such a way as will show whether they have clearly understood, and fixed in their memories what they have been learning. The notes were originally written for the normal pupils; but as they may be of some use to the teaaher, I have had them printed with the lessons.

It may be well to say that the school has never been connected with any church or association;—the word mission is used in a general sense, and the name was given to it because it was established at a time when so little encouragement was given to this branch of industrial education, that any work connected with it might properly be called "mission" work. It was the first, or one of the first, free schools of cookery established in this country, and as I was particularly interested in the introduction of cookery into the public school system, classes of girls were invited after school hours for many years, until the first class was detailed three years ago. They were not only interested themselves, but they took pains to interest others, and have done their share in forwarding the cause of industrial education. As it seems better now that the lessons should be committed to memory, I have decided to have them printed; leaving them just as they were written, and in the same simple language in which they were given to the girls.

A. L. W.

1205 G Street, Washington, D. C.

MANUAL OF COOKERY.

Lesson 1.

In making a fire, first clear the grate, and brush off the stove, taking up all the ashes nicely into an old coal-hod. Then open the main dampers above and below, put in the paper or shavings, and on them lay the pieces of kindling wood lightly across each other so that the air may pass through. Scatter in a little coal, and light the paper with a match. Add more coal slowly, until the fire is well kindled, then close the lower drafts, and half-close the upper one, and you will have a steady fire, and more heat, than you would if you let it burn up very hot at first. No range or stove should be allowed to get red hot, and the coal should never come above the fire-bricks, as it checks the heat from passing to the oven, and to the top of the stove, and also warps the covers. In winter, always see that the water pipes are not frozen, as it is dangerous to light a fire if there is a boiler connected with them; and never use coal-oil on or near a fire, or in lighting one. Placing paper on the top as well as at the bottom in kindling a fire, and lighting both, will make it less apt to smoke. Soft pine wood split into small pieces, is best for kindling, and white ash coal is used for stoves, while Lorberry, or red ash coal should be used in ranges. An old dust brush should be kept for use on the range and hearth. The hands should always be nicely washed before beginning to cook, and the head should be protected by a cap, or covering of some kind.

TIP-TOP BISCUIT.

Sift one quart of flour. Add two full teaspoonfuls of baking powder, and one teaspoonful of salt, and sift it again. Rub one large tablespoonful of butter through the flour, and then stir in slowly with a spoon, one cup of sweet milk, or enough to make a soft dough. Flour the bread board, and turn the dough onto it with the spoon. Toss it lightly from side to side a few times with a knife, and then roll it out about one-half of an inch thick, and cut into very small round biscuit. Place one-half of these in the pan, and rub the top of each with a little milk; then place the others on top of them, and bake in a quick oven for twenty minutes. These biscuit should not be larger than a half-dollar, and can be cut with the cover of a small tin box. They can also be made richer with a little more butter, and baked as single biscuit. In this case, make of the usual size.

NOTES FOR THE TEACHER.

Show the pupils how to mix and handle dough lightly and quickly; letting each one in turn have a lesson in rolling and cutting. For a class of twelve girls make the whole quantity which is given in the recipe; and detail one or two girls to watch the biscuit in the oven, while others wash the dishes, and prepare the room for the next class; showing them how to do everything very nicely.

The teacher may think it best to have a preparatory lesson on the first day of school, and in that case, after the names of the pupils have been entered in the class-book, let them have a short lesson on the various kinds of cooking utensils; and also make the ginger snaps which are given in the twenty-first lesson, as they are interesting and easily made.

Lesson 2.

Hot ashes should never be put into anything which is made of wood, as it might cause a dangerous fire. When cool, they should be sifted, and the cinders should be picked out carefully, and used after dinner or when there is no baking or ironing to be done. An open door or window opposite a stove will often deaden a fire, or make it smoke when first lighted. The upper main damper should always be left a little open in order to let off the coal-gas. After the breakfast is entirely cooked, put on coal, and keep the stove closed unless you have to bake bread, in which case the oven dampers must be arranged for that. A clear, steady fire is needed for baking, and the simplest way to test an oven is to touch it with your finger, wet in cold water; if it hisses loudly, it is hot enough for bread. It is important to learn thoroughly how to manage every different stove or range, either from printed directions or from some one who understands it; as a damper must be pulled out to heat some ovens, while others are heated by pushing in the damper. The soot should be cleaned out from under and around the oven once a week with the scraper which comes for that purpose; and the other flues should be cleaned occasionally.

Stove polish should be moistened with water in an old

dish, and this with the brushes should be kept together in one fixed place. The polish should be put all over the cold stove with a rag, and brushed in thoroughly while wet. Then polish it with the dry brush, when the stove is a little warm. The early morning is therefore the best time to do it; but otherwise it is best to black it at night when the stove is a little warm. Stoves are generally blacked every day; but they can be kept very nice by blacking them two or three times a week, if care is taken to wipe off everything which drops on them.

SUGAR COOKIES.

One cup of sugar; half a cup of butter closely packed; two eggs; one and a half tablespoonfuls of milk; one-quarter of a teaspoonful of ginger; half a teaspoonful of grated nutmeg; and three full cups of flour with two teaspoonfuls of baking powder in it. Cream the butter in a bowl with a wooden spoon; and then stir the sugar thoroughly into it. Break in the eggs one at a time, and beat the mixture well. Then add the milk and spice, and sift in the flour and baking powder gradually. Butter the pans, and roll out the dough about an eighth of an inch thick on a floured board. Cut out the cookies with a hole in the centre, and bake them a light brown in a quick oven.

These cookies may be rolled a little thicker, and some caraway seeds can be mixed with the dough; or they may be made a little richer and rolled very thin.

NOTES FOR THE TEACHER.

Make half the quantity given in the recipe, and let the pupils practice rolling, cutting and baking. Explain to them also the management of an oven, and how to prepare a fire for baking. If in any of the lessons there should be a little unoccupied time, it can be filled by showing the pupils how to black the stove, or polish the tinware, or arrange the dressers and closets nicely, or by questioning them on the previous lessons.

Lesson 3.

There are two kinds of white flour, the old process flour, which should be used for cake or pastry, and the new process flour which should be used for bread. The best flour is the cheapest in the end, and should be kept in a dry place. If it should happen to get damp, it must be dried before it is used. If you wish the bread to be moist and tender, make a soft dough, and knead it only five or ten minutes; but fine-grained, dry bread requires a stiff dough, and should be kneaded twenty minutes or more. In kneading dough on the bread board, pat it lightly and do not press it down. Let all motion be as elastic as possible, and work it so as as to keep the same smooth side always on the board. Use as little flour as possible on the bread board, as bread, cake and pastry are made tough by flour added in that way; and for the same reason it is best to cut as many cakes as possible from each rolling of the dough.

Bread and rolls should be made with cold water in summer, and put in a cool place to rise. In winter they should be made with lukewarm water, and put in a warm place to rise. The bowl or pan should be closely covered with a thick cloth kept for that purpose; and a wooden or tin cover should be placed on top of this, as it will make it air tight, and prevent a crust from forming on the dough. They should be covered in the same way, when set to rise in the pans in the morning. Bread should stand for an hour in the pan, and rolls should stand for an hour and a half; but they can be hurried by putting them in a warm place. A hotter oven is required for rolls than for bread. Always watch carefully whatever you are baking in the oven, and turn or move it as is required. All yeast should be fresh and sweet, and half a cup of baker's, or of home-made yeast, will raise two quarts of flour. If part of a cake of Fleischman's yeast is left unused, it can be wrapped tightly in the tin-foil, and will remain good for a day or two if kept in a cool place.

PLAIN BREAD.

Sift two quarts of flour with one full teaspoonful of salt in it; and then rub into it well one tablespoonful of butter or lard. Dissolve one-third of a cake of Fleischman's yeast, in a cup of lukewarm water, with one even tablespoonful of sugar, and add it to the flour. Then add carefully water enough to make a soft dough, stirring it all the time. When well mixed, flour the bread board, and turn the dough onto it. Knead it five or ten minutes, and then put it back into the bowl, covering it closely. Set it to rise, and in the morning turn the dough as early as possible onto a floured board, and knead it about five minutes. Then put it into well buttered pans, filling carefully all the corners, and evening the top. Cover it closely and set it to rise until it is ready to go into the oven. Bread should always be thoroughly baked, and have a light brown crust. The loaves should be taken from the pan at once and wrapped in a clean towel. Then stand them on end, resting them against a sieve or pan, as hot bread should never be laid flat on the table.

NOTES FOR THE TEACHER.

Before the dictation is given, show the pupils how to shape the different kinds of rolls from dough which has been prepared beforehand either by the teacher or by another class, and then put them to rise in a pan in a warm place, so that the girls can bake them before they leave. After the lesson has been dictated, make one-half of the quantity of dough given in the recipe, and leave it to rise in the bowl. If several classes are following each other, one class can sometimes bake the dough which another has mixed.

Lesson 4.

Soup stock should be made in a large, tightly covered kettle. To every pound of meat or bone allow one quart of cold water, one even teaspoonful of salt, and half a teaspoonful of pepper. Whether cooked or uncooked, the meat should always be cut into small pieces, and the bones should be broken in order to let the marrow come out easily. Let the meat stand in the water until it is slightly colored with the juice, and then let it come slowly to a boil, removing every particle of scum as it rises, or the soup will look and taste unpleasantly. A cup of cold water thrown in will cause the scum to rise more readily. Let it boil gently and steadily, allowing an hour to every pound of meat. The water will boil down to about one-third of the original quantity, and the cover of the kettle can be left a little off during the last half hour, if it does not boil down fast enough. When done, strain it into a bowl or stone jar kept for the purpose. In winter it will become a thick jelly, but even if it remains liquid it can be used. The cake of fat which forms on the top should be left on until you are ready to use the stock. This fat, when melted and strained, can be used instead of lard for many purposes, if the stock is made from beef only. The jelly can be melted into a strong, clear soup, or it can be diluted with an equal quantity of water and made into vegetable or other soups, or a little of it can be used in making various gravies. White stock is made from veal and poultry. If a stock-pot is kept at the back of the stove, it should frequently be entirely emptied and washed out.

BOILED POTATOES.

Select potatoes, if possible, which are of the same size, but if some should happen to be larger than others, they can be cut in halves. They may be boiled either with or without their skins, but in either case they should be nicely washed. The skin of new potatoes can be rubbed off with a coarse towel, but old potatoes should be peeled with a sharp knife, cutting out carefully all the black specks. Let them lie in cold water for several hours, and then put them on the fire, with water enough to cover them well, allowing one teaspoonful of salt to every quart of water. New potatoes should always be put into boiling water, but old ones may be put on either in cold or boiling water. They should be cooked about half an hour. When they are tender, pour off every drop of water, sprinkle them with a little salt and shake them lightly. Set the saucepan at the back of the stove and cover it with a clean towel or with the cover, which should be left a little off. They should be taken from the saucepan singly with a spoon.

DRAWN BUTTER.

Melt two ounces (or two full tablespoonfuls) of butter in a saucepan, and stir into it gradually one tablespoonful of flour until perfectly smooth. Then slowly add half a pint of hot water and a very little salt, and let it cook for a minute or two till it thickens, stirring constantly.

For rich drawn butter, take four ounces of butter and the same quantity of flour and of water.

NOTES FOR THE TEACHER.

The soup stock is not made in this lesson. The potatoes should be put in water before the pupils come, so that they may put them on the fire before the dictation is given. Then let them have a lesson in mashing potatoes, and in potato snow; and make the drawn butter. Explain to them also what a stock-pot is.

Lesson 5.

Water is boiling when there is active motion, and bubbles rise to the top and throw off steam. As the water boils more or less violently, this motion will be proportionately greater or less. When the bubbles remain underneath the surface, the water is simmering; water enough to last through the whole time of cooking should be put in at first, and if any is added, it should be actually boiling. Never let anything stop boiling even for a minute; and never let anything boil very fast, as steady, gentle cooking will make meat and vegetables tender, and is better for everything. Meat which is to be used for soup should be put on in cold water; but meat which is to be boiled for dinner should be put on in boiling water so that the juices may be kept in.

Soup should be skimmed before the vegetables are put in. It may be strained clear into the tureen, or thickened by mashing through some of the vegetables, or it may be served without straining at all, merely taking out the bone. White soups are made from white meats, such as veal and chicken, or from oysters, and should be as colorless as possible. Brown soups are made from the dark meats, and may be colored with a little caramel. Toasted bread cut into small square pieces, is often served with clear soup. Vegetables which are to be put into soup should be nicely washed and prepared as each one may require. A little bouquet of dried herbs, with a bay-leaf in it is often boiled in soup, and should be taken out before serving it.

VEGETABLE SOUP.

Dilute two quarts of jellied soup stock with one pint of water. Add to it one small parsnip, one small carrot, one small turnip, and two small onions, all chopped fine. Also half a cupful of chopped cabbage, three tomatoes peeled and sliced, or half a pint of canned ones, and half a cupful of chopped celery, or half a teaspoonful of celery salt. Boil gently for one hour, and then add half a teaspoonful of pepper, one saltspoonful of ground cloves, and a little salt. Boil a few minutes longer and serve without straining. The vegetables can be varied or omitted according to taste, and a spoonful of barley or rice can be added if desired.

This soup can be made from a roast beef bone or from soup meat, but the meat should be boiled for some time before the vegetables are put in, and should be put on the fire several hours before dinner.

BOSTON BROWN BREAD.

Six ounces of yellow corn meal; four ounces of rye meal; one ounce of white flour; one even teaspoonful of salt; one even teaspoonful of soda; half a pint of milk; two large spoonfuls (half a gill) of molasses; and water enough to make quite a stiff dough.

Sift the two kinds of meal together, and then sift in the flour and salt. Add the molasses, the milk, and the soda (dissolved in a little hot water), and lastly add as much water as is required. Fill the tin about three quarters full, and fasten the cover on tight. Put it into a closed kettle with enough boiling water in it to nearly cover the tin and let it steam steadily four hours. This bread can be made without milk, or with sour milk, in which case the soda is put into the milk. If a firm crust is desired, the bread can be put into the oven for a short time, after taking it from the steamer.

CARAMEL.

Melt half a pound of loaf, or brown sugar in a small frying pan, with one teaspoonful of water. Stir steadily over the fire till it becomes a dark brown color. Then add slowly one cup of boiling water, and one teaspoonful of salt. Boil a minute longer. After it has cooled, put it in a bottle, and keep it tightly corked. One tablespoonful will color clear soup; and a teaspoonful of it is used in some kinds of gravy.

NOTES FOR THE TEACHER.

The stock must be prepared beforehand, and the soup with the vegetables should be put on the fire before the dictation is given, so that it may be ready before the class leaves. One-half of the quantity given in the recipe will be sufficient, and a little of the caramel can be used in it. If several classes are following each other rapidly, it will not be possible to make the brown bread, but the pupils might be shown how to roll and sift bread crumbs, or any other simple thing which may occur to the teacher.

Lesson 6.

Green vegetables should be fresh and firm, and should be nicely washed before they are cooked. If they are to be put into boiling water, let it be freshly boiled for the purpose, and allow one teaspoonful of salt to a quart of water. They should be cooked until tender, and this can only be found out by watching and testing them with a fork, as no exact time can be given. For most vegetables, about half an hour is required, but as they grow older they require more cooking than when they are young and tender. They retain their color better if cooked quickly and uncovered.

If tomatoes are to be eaten raw, they should be peeled like any other vegetable or fruit, and may be served whole, with salad dressing, or cut into slices and dressed with a little pepper, salt and vinegar. In either case they should be put into the ice chest for a time. If they are to be cooked, pour boiling water on them, and let them stand for a time before peeling them. They may be sliced and fried in a little hot butter, dredging them first with a little salt, pepper, and flour. They can also be broiled, baked, or stewed. Canned tomatoes should never be left in the tin-can after it has been opened. If there is more than will be used at once, pour it out into a bowl, before putting it away. In buying canned goods, great care should be taken to select the best, as the others are often unwholesome, and even dangerous.

MOCK BISQUE.

One quart of tomatoes; three pints of milk; two heaping tablespoonfuls of flour; two tablespoonfuls of butter; one full teaspoonful of salt; one scant teaspoonful of pepper and one scant teaspoonful of soda.

Put the tomato on the fire in a saucepan, and when it boils, add the soda and let it boil ten minutes, stirring occasionally. Then strain it into a bowl, through a sieve fine enough to keep back the seeds. In the meantime put the milk on in a double boiler, and cream the butter in a bowl. Then mix the flour well with the butter, and afterwards stir slowly into it one cupful of the hot milk. When the rest of the milk boils, pour this mixture into it very slowly and stir till it thickens, which will be in about five minutes. Add the pepper and salt, and the strained tomato, and serve at once.

SAUCES.

The foundation of most sauces is what is known as a roux, which is made by melting some butter in a saucepan, and stirring into it a little dry flour, until the mixture is perfectly smooth.

Many different sauces can be made by adding to this a little hot water, hot milk, or stock, and other ingredients of various kinds. A cream sauce is made by pouring slowly on the roux hot cream or hot milk; and this, and sauces made from white stock are called white sauces. When the butter and flour are allowed to brown, it is called a brown roux, and brown sauces are made from it by using brown stock, and various seasonings.

BOILED RICE.

Wash clean one cupful of rice and put it into a saucepan

with one quart of water and a teaspoonful of salt, and boil it until quite tender ; then turn it into a colander to drain without stirring it at all. Let it stand in a warm place to dry for five or ten minutes befor serving. Every kernel of rice should be separate, dry, and look very white.

NOTES FOR THE TEACHER.

Let the pupils pick over and wash the rice, and put it on to boil as soon as they come. After the dictation they can make the mock bisque ; and the roux and sauces are not made in this lesson. Explain to them also that this soup is called mock bisque, because it resembles lobster bisque in taste and color. It is very nice and can be quickly made if soup is wanted unexpectedly.

Lesson 7.

Saucepans and kettles should never be filled entirely full, for the water would constantly boil over ; nor should they ever be left on the fire without any water at all in them, as they would soon be burnt through and ruined. A double boiler should be used for milk, custard, oatmeal, and anything which burns easily. When milk bubbles a little in a double boiler, it is boiling. When cooked in this way, it will never burn nor boil over. The water in the under boiler should be boiling when the upper one is put in, and should be filled up with boiling water, if it is used for a long time.

Potatoes, rice, oatmeal, and many other things can be cooked very nicely in a steamer placed over a kettte of boiling water. A tea-kettle should be washed, and filled fresh every morning, or it will soon give an unpleasant taste to the tea or coffee. The water from a range boiler should never be used for cooking; fresh water for this purpose should be kept in a clean kettle on the stove.

CORN STARCH BLANC MANGE

Measure out one pint of milk. Dissolve two tablespoonfuls of corn starch in about half a cupful of it. Put the remainder of the milk on the fire in a double boiler, and add to it one stick of cinnamon, two tablespoonfuls of sugar, one-third of a saltspoonful of salt, and heat till nearly boiling Then add the mixed corn starch slowly, and let it boil four minutes, stirring all the time. Take out the cinnamon, and pour the cornstarch into a mould, or into small cups, which should first be wet with cold water. When cold and stiff, turn it onto a dish, and serve with sugar and milk; or with custard, or any kind of jelly or preserved fruit put round it on the dish. This blanc mange can be made with eggs if preferred.

POACHED EGGS.

Fill a deep frying pan nearly full of hot water with a teaspoonful of salt in it, and let it boil gently. Break each egg into a saucer, and slide it slowly into the water, letting it cook by itself, and pouring a little of the water gently over it with a teaspoon. When done, lift it out with a skimmer, and place it on a slice of hot buttered toast, sprinkling it with a little pepper and salt, and trimming the edges nicely. The toast may be dry, or wet by dipping it quickly into hot water. One or two tablespoonfuls of vinegar are sometimes put into the water in which eggs are poached.

YEAST.

Wash and pare three small potatoes, and lay them in cold water. Put one tablespoonful of loose hops to steep, in a pint of boiling water. In about half an hour mix together in a large bowl one tablespoonful of flour, two teaspoonfuls of sugar, and one full teaspoonful of salt. Grate the potato into this. Let the hops boil for a minute, and then strain them through a sieve onto the potato and flour, stirring it constantly and quickly. If it does not thicken, put it back on the fire, and let it boil a few moments, still stirring as before. When lukewarm, add half a cup of yeast, or half a cake of Fleischman's yeast dissolved in a little warm sweetened water. Let it rise until it is light, and keep it in a cool place, in a tightly corked jug.

NOTES FOR THE TEACHER.

Let the pupils make the blanc mange as soon as they come; mould it in small baking cups, and set it in a cold place. Then give the lesson, and poach some eggs; and by that time the blanc mange will be stiff enough to be turned out. Serve it with a little jelly. Show them also how to use a pitcher, or a tin pail, set into a pan with hot water in it, if they have no double boiler. It is better to raise the pail on two or three muffin rings if possible.

Lesson 8.

Eggs should always be kept in a cool place; and when they are used, do not forget to save some of the egg shells for clearing coffee. In breaking eggs, it is better to break each one singly over a cup, because one bad egg will oblige you to throw away all which have been previously broken. If an egg is fresh and good, the white will rise up clear and firm from the shell. In separating the whites from the yolks, if a little of the yolk should get in with the whites, it can be taken out with a piece of eggshell, as it will adhere to the inside; or it can be taken out with the corner of a clean towel twisted into a point and dampened. In beating eggs with an egg-whisk or fork, keep the upper arm quiet and close to the side, and beat with the wrist. A Dover egg-beater is very good for the yolks, or for whole eggs, but should never be used for the whites of eggs, as it breaks the fibres two much. A Dover egg-beater should be kept in gentle motion round the bowl, and should never be held steadily on the bottom. The handle should be washed as seldom as possible, and the little wheels should be oiled occasionally or they will wear out. In beating sugar and the whites of eggs together, it is better to add the sugar slowly, for as eggs vary in size it is not possible to give the exact quantity of sugar required. The usual proportion for a meringue is three tablespoonfuls of powdered sugar to the whites of five eggs, and they should be beaten until very stiff. A pudding should be cooled a little before the meringue is put on, and should then be browned slightly in the oven. Cream puffs, ice-cream, and puddings which have eggs, milk, sugar, and lemon or other flavorings in them, should be eaten while fresh, as they become very unwholesome, and dangerous if kept too long. The juice of fresh fruits is always far better than any extract, and none but the best extracts should be used, as the cheaper ones are not always reliable.

BOILED CUSTARD.

One quart of milk; five tablespoonfuls of sugar; two whole eggs, and the yolks of six more; one teaspoonful of lemon or vanilla extract, or half a teaspoonful of almond extract.

Boil the milk in a double boiler, and take it from the stove. Beat the eggs and sugar together and then pour the milk slowly into them, stirring constantly. Put the mixture back on the fire in the double boiler, and stir rapidly till it begins to thicken and coats the spoon, which will be in about five minutes. Take it quickly from the fire, and set it in a pan of cold water for a time, and when cool, add the flavoring extract. Custard will curdle if cooked too long. It should be served cold in glass cups.

Very nice custard can be made by using from four to six whole eggs, or by using eight yolks without any whites. Many persons strain custard through a fine sieve, but it is not absolutely necessary.

MERINGUE.

Beat the whites of the six eggs with two or three tablespoonfuls of powdered sugar, until they are very stiff, and put a little on the top of each custard.

BOILED MACARONI.

Macaroni should never be soaked or washed. Break about a quarter of a pound into pieces from three to four inches long, and drop them slowly into a kettle full of well salted boiling water. When quite tender put them into a colander to drain. In the meantime boil one pint of milk with a small piece of butter, and thicken it with a teaspoonful of flour made into a paste with cold water. Put in the macaroni and let it simmer a short time before serving it. Allow an hour or more for the first boiling of the macaroni, as it should be thoroughly cooked.

NOTES FOR THE TEACHER.

Make the whole quantity of custard, and let the pupils cook it before the lesson is given. The meringue can be made afterwards. Half of the quantity of macaroni can be cooked and should be put on early; or it can be entirely omitted. Tell them that it is better to use whole eggs for custard, unless it is wanted for some special occasion.

Lesson 9.

When we immerse and cook anything in very hot or as it is commonly called "boiling" fat, we fry it; and when we cook it in a spider or saucepan, with a little melted butter or lard, we sauter it. Cooking on a griddle or slightly greased pan is baking, and griddle cakes are therefore baked and not fried. A kettle should be filled about half or two-thirds full of fat, and when it is very hot a blue smoke will rise from it. If a bit of bread dropped in will brown quickly, the fat is hot enough to cook with. The heat of the fat should be watched and regulated just as carefully as the heat of an oven is, as the lightest dough will be made heavy if the fat is not just right. It should be allowed to heat up occasionally, and there should never be more than three or four doughnuts or fish balls in the kettle at a time, for the fat will be chilled and make them heavy, and they will also "soak the fat," as it is called, and be greasy. If they are put in gently with a ladle, the fat will not spatter and burn the hand. A kettle of hot fat should always be placed carefully where it cannot be upset; and no cold water, nor anything which is wet with water, should ever be put into it as the fat will spatter dangerously.

DOUGHNUTS.

Cream thoroughly one large tablespoonful of butter, and work into it one heaping cup of fine brown sugar. Add to this three or four eggs and beat them all together with two teaspoonfuls of ground cinnamon, and one teaspoonful of nutmeg. Then add one cupful of sour milk with one teaspoonful of soda in it (or enough to sweeten it.) Lastly sift in about two pints and a half of flour. Make a soft dough, and roll it on the bread-board about half an inch thick. Cut into cakes with a hole in the centre, and fry in a kettle of boiling lard. Take them out with a skimmer, and put them in a colander to drain. A little powdered sugar should be sifted over them.

They can be made with one cup of sweet milk, and two teaspoonfuls of baking powder sifted in with the flour.

SARATOGA CHIPS.

Pare and wash two or three potatoes, and cut out the black specks. Then slice them as thin as wafers with a sharp knife and lay them in very cold water over night. In the morning dry them thoroughly with a towel, and drop a few slices at a time into a kettle of boiling lard. Fry them to a light golden brown, and then take them out with a skimmer and lay them on brown paper in a pan. Sprinkle them with a little salt, and set them in the oven a minute to dry. They can be served either hot or cold.

NOTES FOR THE TEACHER.

One large potato should be prepared and put in cold water by the class before the lesson is given. Make one-half the quantity given in the recipe for doughnuts, and fry them before the Saratoga chips are fried. The pupils might be told of the different kinds of fat which can be used for frying, and also how to clarify uncooked fat.

Lesson 10.

Lard which has been used for frying should never be left in the kettle; when it has cooled a little, dip it out with a small tin dipper, and strain it through a fine wire strainer into a tin pail kept for the purpose. If codfish balls or any article which would give an unpleasant taste to the fat have been fried in it, put the fat when cold with three tablespoonfuls of cold water in a kettle on the fire. When it gets hot it will bubble, and after the bubbling ceases, and a blue smoke rises, put in a raw potato which has been peeled and sliced. When the potato is done it should be taken out, and the fat will be clarified. By treating it in this way, and adding fresh lard, the same fat can be used for a long time, but should occasionally be thrown away entirely.

CODFISH BALLS.

Boil in salted water eight or nine medium sized potatoes, and mash them lightly. Let them cool, and in the meantime pick one pound of salt fish into fine strips, being careful to take out every bone. Pour on enough boiling water to cover the fish, and let it stand ten minutes. Then drain it through a colander, and squeeze it well in the hands; put it in a wooden tray and pound it with a potato masher until all the fibres are separated. Mix it thoroughly with one large quart of the mashed potato, and add one tablespoonful of butter, two eggs, half a teaspoonful of pepper, and a little salt if required. Make it quite soft with milk, and shape with the hands into small round balls. Fry two or three at a time in a kettle of boiling lard. Take them out with a skimmer, and drain them on soft brown paper. One teaspoonful of onion juice, one teaspoonful of lemon juice, and a quarter of a teaspoonful of celery salt can be added if desired.

If the fish is very salt, boiling water should be poured on a second time, and the mixture of fish and potato should always be tasted and seasoned rightly before the balls are shaped. If the potatoes are cool, a larger quantity of milk can be used than when they are warm, and this will make the fish balls more delicate.

NOTES FOR THE TEACHER.

One-half the quantity given in the recipe will make enough balls for a large class. They should be made as soft as possible, and yet stiff enough to retain their shape after being moulded, and should be fried an even rich brown color.

Lesson 11.

A frying pan should always be well heated before the butter or lard is put into it. This should not be allowed to melt entirely, and should be put in a moment only before it is to be used, as it will turn brown if allowed to stand. A little lard or butter for greasing pans should be kept in a small dish, and used for nothing else.

A soapstone griddle is considered the best, and it should never be greased. A new iron griddle can be cleaned with sapolio, and if it is rough, put it on the stove and rub it well with some dry salt. A griddle should be well heated before it is greased, and should be greased again between each set of cakes with a piece of clean brown paper or a white rag, using no more lard or butter than for baking pans. If there is too much grease, the cakes will be heavy round the edge. Some persons prefer to use butter for everything, and the pans for bread or cake should always be buttered; but for griddle cakes, and for cooking over cold potatoes or cold mush, lard is generally preferred, as they will be dryer, and of a better color when cooked with it, and are also less apt to burn. Care should be taken also to scrape off at once any little pieces that may happen to fall on a pan or griddle, for they will burn and smoke whatever is being cooked. The bowl with the batter in it should be held close to the griddle, and just enough of the batter to make one cake should be taken up in the spoon, having first stirred it well from the bottom each time, and scraped in what has collected on the side of the bowl. Clean the bottom of the spoon on the edge of the bowl, and pour the batter from the point of it. Griddle cakes should be small, round, and of uniform size, and should always be served very hot.

CORNMEAL SLAPPERS.

Mix together one pint of cornmeal, one teaspoonful of butter, one teaspoonful of sugar, and one teaspoonful of salt. Pour onto the mixture enough boiling water to wet the meal. Let it cool, and add two well beaten eggs, and cold milk enough to make a thin batter. Bake in small thin cakes on a griddle.

SCRAMBLED EGGS.

Break six eggs into a bowl, and beat them a minute or two. Then stir into them about two-thirds of a cupful of milk, with a scant teaspoonful of salt, and half a teaspoonful of pepper. Partially melt a tablespoonful of butter in a well heated frying pan, and pour in the mixture slowly, stirring it lightly with a fork until it has thickened. Then turn it at once into a hot dish. When done, it should have the consistency of a baked custard.

NOTES FOR THE TEACHER.

The whole quantity given in the recipe for cornmeal

slappers should be made, so that each pupil in turn may bake a few cakes. Show them also how to mix batter quickly and neatly, without letting it collect on the side of the bowl. The recipe for scrambled eggs can be halved, and a smaller frying pan should be used than when the whole quantity is taken.

Lesson 12.

One quart of flour is one pound.
One pint of granulated sugar is one pound.
Two cups of packed butter are one pound.
Ten eggs are one pound.
Two cups and a half of powdered sugar are one pound.
Four cups of flour are one pound.
Three cups of meal are one pound.
One heaping tablespoonful of granulated sugar is one ounce.
Two full tablespoonfuls of powdered sugar are one ounce.
One full tablespoonful of butter is one ounce.
Two full tablespoonfuls of flour are one ounce.
Two full tablespoonfuls of coffee are one ounce.
One pint of chopped meat closely packed is one pound.

LIQUID MEASURE.

Four saltspoonfuls make one teaspoonful.
Four teaspoonfuls make one tablespoonful.
Two tablespoonfuls make one ounce.

Four tablespoonfuls make one wineglassful, or half a gill.
Eight tablespoonfuls or four ounces make a gill.
Four gills make a pint.
Two pints make a quart.

BREAD FRITTERS—No. 1.

Take a stale loaf of baker's bread and cut it into half-inch slices. Beat up three eggs, and stir into them a pint of milk and a saltspoonful of salt. Dip the slices into the milk and egg and lay them into a deep dish; pour over them the rest of the milk and egg, and let them soak till tender. Then sauter them in a little butter, turning them over so that each side may be of a light brown color. Serve hot at breakfast with syrup, or sugar and butter.

BREAD FRITTERS—No. 2.

Cut a stale loaf of baker's bread into half-inch slices and trim off the hard crusts evenly. Beat up three eggs, and stir into them one pint of milk, a saltspoonful of salt, and a tablespoonful of flour made into a paste with a little cold water. Dip each slice of bread into a little milk to moisten it, and then dip it into the batter, and either sauter them in butter (browning on both sides), or fry them in boiling lard. Serve hot as a dessert with a hot sweet sauce.

PLAIN OMELET.

Beat the yolks of four eggs with a Dover egg beater (or any good one) and add two tablespoonfuls of milk and one teaspoonful of salt. Beat the whites very light with an egg whisk, and cut the yolks thoroughly into them. Have an omelet pan very hot, and put in a tablespoonful of butter, then pour in the beaten egg. Shake the pan vigorously on the hottest part of the stove until the egg begins to thicken, and then let it stand a minute or two to brown. Run a knife between the two sides of the omelet and the pan; fold over on itself, and turn into a dish. Serve at once.

The eggs can be beaten whole, if preferred, without separating the yolks and whites. A little chopped parsely, or chopped ham, or chopped tomato can be used in an omelet.

NOTES FOR THE TEACHER.

Let the pupils make one kind of fritters and an omelet; and show them how to separate nicely the yolks and whites of the eggs. Explain to them also what is meant by a "cutting" motion, and show them how it differs from mixing by stirring.

Lesson 13.

Oysters should be entirely fresh, as they become unwholesome if kept too long. The largest oysters should be selected for frying, for pickling, for broiling, and for serving raw. Raw oysters are improved by being laid on ice for a time. They should be sprinkled with salt and pepper, and may be served in a dish or in small single plates, with slices of lemon. Many persons prefer to eat them with vinegar; and cayenne pepper is often used instead of black pepper.

In preparing oysters for cooking, take them out singly with the fingers, feeling carefully for every little piece of shell.

Put them in a bowl, and then strain the liquor and keep it separate. Oysters should be simmered and never boiled hard or cooked long as it will make them tough and small. Oyster liquor should be skimmed when it begins to boil.

In frying oysters, croquettes or anything delicate, a wire basket should be used. A layer of oysters should be placed in the bottom of it, and it should be hung or held in the fat until they are cooked. Then lift it out, remove the oysters, and put in a fresh layer. If any crumbs in which oysters or croquettes have been rolled are left over, they should be thrown away. Oysters sautéd in a little hot butter without crumbs or egg are very nice.

Invalids should never be allowed to eat the hard part of an oyster; and raw oysters are generally more wholesome for them than those which have been cooked, as they are more easily digested.

FRIED OYSTERS.

Drain one quart of oysters thoroughly through a colander, and then take each one out singly and lay it on a clean towel to dry. Beat one egg with half a teaspoonful of salt and a saltspoonful of pepper. Dip the oysters first in cracker crumbs, or bread crumbs, then in the egg, and then in the crumbs again. Drop them gently into the boiling lard with a skimmer, and fry to a light brown; then take them out with a skimmer, lay them on brown paper for a moment, and serve on a hot dish.

OYSTER SOUP.

Put one cup of milk or cream on the fire to boil in a double boiler. Put one quart of oysters in a saucepan with their own strained liquor, and one cup of cold water. The moment they begin to simmer, pour them through a colander into a hot bowl. Melt a tablespoonful of butter in the same saucepan and stir into it with an egg-whisk one tablespoonful of sifted flour. Let this cook one or two minutes, and add the oyster liquor gradually, stirring rapidly as you pour it in. Then add slowly the hot milk, with a few grains of cayenne pepper, a little ground mace and a little salt. Let this all boil up together, then add the oysters, and serve at once.

NOTES FOR THE TEACHER.

The pupils can make the soup and fry the oysters, using either the whole quantity given, or half of it. One pint of oysters will be enough for a small class to fry.

Lesson 14.

When buying fresh meat, select that which has a clear white fat, and firm healthy look. Meat is made more tender by being kept for a time, and mutton is especially improved by it. Fresh meat should never be soaked at all; it can either be washed in cold water, or wiped off with a damp cloth.

The best beef is of a clear, red color, and is slightly marbled with white fat. The sirloin and the sixth, seventh and eighth ribs are the best roasting pieces; the ribs can be removed and used for stock, and the meat can be rolled and skewered, trimming off all the rough bits. The tenderloin cut is the nicest, but is much more expensive than the others.

Mutton also should be of a clear, red color, with white, firm fat; a leg or a shoulder of mutton may be either roasted or boiled. Veal should have white fat, and the flesh should be slightly pink in color. The fillet, breast, and loin are the best pieces for roasting, and the neck and ribs for stewing Pork should have fine, white fat, and the meat should be white and smooth. The spare-rib is considered the most delicate piece for roasting, but the leg, loin, and shoulder are very good. Pork and veal are very nice when cold; they should never be eaten at all in hot weather.

The oven should be very hot when meat is first put in, but may be slackened afterwards. For rare meat, allow ten to twelve minutes to the pound; and allow fifteen to twenty minutes to a pound if the meat is to be well done. Veal, pork and lamb should be thoroughly cooked; while beef and mutton should be left quite rare.

ROAST BEEF.

Sprinkle the beef with a little pepper and salt, and dredge it with flour; put a little water in the baking pan, and place the meat in it on a small rack which fits into the pan, and will keep the meat out of the water. Put it into the oven, and then melt a tablespoonful of butter in a cupful of boilng water. When the flour has browned, baste the meat with this, and continue to do it every fifteen or twenty minutes. Sprinkle it once more with pepper and salt, and dredge it with flour at least twice. When the meat is done, serve it on a hot platter.

GRAVY.

Take all the fat from the drippings, and scrape into the water whatever may have browned onto the sides and bottom of the pan; then pour it into a saucepan, or else set the baking pan on the top of the stove, and let the gravy cook gently. If it is not thick enough, mix a teaspoonful of flour into a smooth paste with a little cold water and add it, and then let it all come to a boil, stirring gently. If the gravy is too light colored, thicken it with burnt flour, or add a little caramel. It is sometimes strained through a sieve, but if it is well mixed and smooth this is not necessary. A little boiling water can be added to the water in the pan, if needed.

COLD BEEF AND CABBAGE.

Chop one head of tender cabbage without the stalks, and put it in a saucepan with two tablespoonfuls of butter, one saltspoonful of salt, and half a saltspoonful of pepper, and stir it occasionally until it is quite tender. In the meantime cut some cold meat into neat slices; put them in a frying pan with a tablespoonful of butter and brown them. Lay them in the centre of a hot dish, with the cabbage around them.

NOTES FOR THE TEACHER.

A piece of solid beef weighing not much over a pound can ofter be obtained at the butcher's, and used for a lesson in roasting. It should be prepared and put in the oven before the lesson is given. In every school-room there should be charts showing the different parts of the animal, and how they should look when dressed, and ready to serve; these should be shown and explained to the pupils while they are waiting for the meat to be done, and then they can make the gravy. They should be told also that the most wholesome gravies are made from stock either prepared beforehand, or made for the purpose, by boiling some meat and bone in water with a little salt in it for several hours, and straining it before it is thickened and seasoned.

Lesson 15.

The porter-house and sirloin beefsteaks are the best, and they should always be broiled. Steaks from the round can be either stewed, sautéd, or rolled up with stuffing and baked. The third and fourth cuts of the round are the best for steaks.

Mutton and veal chops and pork chops can be broiled, fried, or sautéd. Veal cutlets can be broiled, sauted, or rolled up with stuffing and baked.

If meat has been washed, it should be well dried with a towel before it is fried or broiled, or it will not brown handsomely. Tender meat should never be pounded; but if it is tough, it can be made tender by pounding it lightly with the back of a meat knife, or with the edge of a plate; or by drawing a knife across it in several cross lines on each side, so as to gash it without cutting through. Two bricks can be placed on the top of the stove, and the broiler may be rested on them, if it is necessary to leave it for a minute or two while broiling. The fire should be hot and clear for broiling; but the time required depends on the size and thickness of the steak. From eight to ten minutes will be sufficient for a rare steak; and from ten to fifteen if it is to be well done. The inside of a steak should be rare but not raw.

BROILED BEEFSTEAK.

A beefsteak should be at least half an inch thick, and many persons prefer one which is three-quarters of an inch thick. If there is much fat, trim it off a little, or it will drop on the coals and smoke. Grease the broiler with a little of the fat from the steak, and then place the meat in the centre of it; hold each side over the coals long enough to sear it over, and then cook it until it is properly done, turning it constantly. Have ready a hot platter; before taking the steak from the broiler, sprinkle one side with salt and pepper; lay it with that side down on the platter and salt and pepper the other side. Put some pieces of butter on this upper side, and serve without turning it, and before the butter is entirely melted.

HASH.

Take cold roast beef, or cold corn beef; remove carefully all the bone, gristle, and skin, and take three parts of lean meat to one of fat meat. Add one-third as much of cold potato as there is of meat, a little onion, pepper, and salt, and chop them all together in a wooden tray until they are very fine and well mixed. Then moisten it with cold gravy, or with water and a little piece of butter. Have ready a hot frying pan, in which a tablespoonful of butter has been melted, and spread the meat smoothly over the bottom of it. Let it simmer till a brown crust has formed on the under side without stirring it at all, and then fold it like an omelet, and serve on a hot platter. The hash can be served without folding by turning it whole onto the platter with the brown side up.

NOTES FOR THE TEACHER.

If the pupils broil a steak before the lesson is given, it will be cold enough to be made into hash before they leave. Show them how to broil a steak without putting a fork into it, and tell them that if they prefer to have more gravy, they must put some butter in the bottom of the dish, and turn the hot steak over in it once or twice.

Lesson 16.

It is very important to know how to prepare nice dishes from inexpensive materials, and also from those which have been already cooked. Every clean bone should be put into the stock pot, and all pieces of fat should be nicely tried out and strained, and kept in a jar, to be exchanged for soap, or made into soft soap. Cold meats and vegetables, cold gravies, bread and cake that are a little dry, and cold oatmeal or cornmeal mush can be used in a variety of ways. Many a little clean piece is thrown away which, if properly used, would make some dish richer and more savory; and a little thought and good management in this way will accomplish and save more than would be supposed. In planning a dinner or any meal, it is a good plan always to consider in what way, the food already in the house, can best be worked in. There is a very mistaken impression that economy is meanness, whereas they are very different. To economise is to make the best possible use of what you have, and to make it go as far as possible for your own and other peoples' advantage. A mean person is one who does not or will not use what she has, or get what she needs, when she can afford it and there is no reason why she should not. To deny one's self, and go without things when it is necessary, is very different, and should never be ridiculed as it too often is. Economy and self-denial are praiseworthy, and lead to success in every way; and no one need ever be ashamed of practicing them.

HOW TO WARM COLD MEAT.

Cut the cold meat off in neat slices, and set it away; then put the bone on in cold water enough to cover it well, and add a sliced onion. Let it cook gently for two hours; and about half an hour before dinner strain it and put the liquid back on the stove, adding some cold gravy if you have it, a little salt and pepper, and sifted dried herb, or any seasoning that is preferred; thicken it with a little flour mixed with cold water, and let it just boil for a minute or so, stirring constantly. Then put in the slices of cold meat and let it simmer until the meat is thoroughly warmed through. If there is no cold gravy, a piece of butter should be added in its place. A tablespoonful of ketchup is very nice in the gravy with cold beef, and a tablespoonful of currant jelly with cold mutton.

MUTTON PIE.

Cut some cold roast mutton into neat slices; lay them in a buttered baking dish or nappy; add the cold gravy and a tablespoonful of currant jelly, and dredge in a little flour; cover it with paste, or with a crust of cold rice or mashed potato. If there is not enough gravy, add a little water, pepper, salt and a piece of butter. Bake three-quarters of an hour.

STEWED BEEFSTEAK WITH CARROTS.

Take one and a half pounds of beefsteak from the round, cut them into pieces three or four inches square, and sauter them in a large frying pan with some butter and an onion chopped very fine. Turn the slices of meat occasionally, and when they are well browned on each side, fill the pan with hot water enough to cover the meat well. Add one teaspoonful of salt, half a teaspoonful of pepper, and an even teaspoonful of ground cloves. Scrape and slice a bunch of small carrots and add them. Cover the pan, and let it all cook gently at the side of the stove until tender, which will require two or three hours. The gravy can be thickened with a scant tablespoonful of flour mixed first with a little cold water, if desired.

NOTES FOR THE TEACHER.

Buy some slices of cold roast meat at a restaurant and let the pupils cook them according to the first recipe. They can try the others at their own homes. Let them also make some baking powder biscuit by the recipe given in the first lesson.

Lesson 18.

Potatoes of both kinds are very nice when baked; they should be well washed, put into a hot oven, and baked about an hour. Sweet potatoes should be boiled with their skin on for about three-quarters of an hour. Cold potatoes can be sliced and fried for breakfast, and cold mashed potato can be made into cakes about three-quarters of an inch thick, which may be baked or fried. Cold potatoes may also be cut into dice and warmed in thickened milk with a little piece of butter and some chopped parsley in it.

Green peas should be nicely picked over, and not washed. Put them into salted boiling water, and cook gently about thirty minutes. Drain them through a colander, and add a little butter and salt after they are in the dish.

String beans should be washed, and cut into small pieces, after carefully stringing them and cutting off the ends. Put them into salted boiling water, and cook about an hour; drain through a colander, and dress with butter and salt.

After removing the tough skin from the white part of asparagus, tie it in bunches, and stand them on end in salted boiling water which should cover the white part well. Cook about twenty minutes, and serve it on some thin slices of buttered toast which have been dipped in the water in which the asparagus was boiled. Sprinkle a little salt over it and add a few small pieces of butter.

Summer squashes or cymlings should be cut up without being peeled, but the seeds should be taken out unless they are very young. Steam till tender, and then mash through a colander, and add a little pepper, salt, sugar and a small piece of butter.

Winter squashes should be cut into pieces, removing all the seeds and fibres. Then pare the pieces and cook them in a steamer for about two hours. When tender, mash fine, and add a heaping tablespoonful of butter, a teaspoonful of salt, a teaspoonful of sugar, and half a teaspoonful of pepper. If there is any cold squash left, it can be mixed with batter the next day, and fried in cakes or fritters.

Turnips should be washed and pared. They may be cut into quarters and cooked for about an hour in salted boiling water; drain them and let them stand a few minutes; then mash them, adding a little salt, pepper, sugar, and a small piece of butter. They may also be cooked and served whole with a white sauce, or with a little butter and pepper. They should be served very hot.

Cabbage should be very carefully washed and laid in cold water for an hour or more; then cut it into quarters and cook it in well-salted boiling water until tender. Take it up and drain it, and serve it without cutting it up any more, and with a little pepper, salt and butter. Cabbage is generally boiled with a piece of corned beef, and in that case, dress it with a little pepper when served, as the butter and salt are not needed.

Parsnips and salsify (oyster plant) should be washed and scraped, and boiled in salted water until tender. They may be cut into slices and served with a white sauce poured over them, or they may be cut lengthwise, and after they are cool, the slices can be fried in a little butter, or rolled in egg and crumbs and fried.

Carrots should be washed, scraped, and boiled in salted water until tender; then cut them into slices and serve with white sauce over them, or with a little pepper and butter.

Beets should be well washed, but never peeled or even pricked, for they will lose their color. They should be put into salted boiling water, and cooked from two to four hours, according to their age When they are boiled, lay them into cold water for two or three minutes, and then rub off the skin. They may be served whole or cut into slices: dress them with a little salt, pepper, and butter. If any are left over, they can be sliced and laid in vinegar and used the next day. Winter beets should be soaked over night if they are tough.

PARSNIP FRITTERS.

Boil three large parsnips in salted water for an hour and a half (or longer if they are not tender); and mash them fine, with half a tablespoonful of butter. Beat two eggs well, and add a third of a cup of milk, half a teaspoonful of salt, one saltspoonful of pepper, and two even tablespoonfuls of flour, mixing them until smooth; then stir thoroughly into the parsnips, and drop by the spoonful into a little hot butter in a frying pan; browning each fritter well on both sides.

Egg plant and oyster plant fritters are made in the same way.

FRITTER BATTER.

Beat two eggs in a bowl and add one tablespoonful of butter (melted), one saltspoonful of salt, half a pint of milk, and about four tablespoonfuls of flour, or enough to make a drop batter. Beat this with an egg-whisk, until very light and smooth, and use at once. This batter may be used with any kind of fruit, or with oysters and clams either whole or chopped.

APPLE FRITTERS.

Peel and core several good sized sour apples, and cut them into slices ; dip each slice into batter, and fry a golden brown in hot fat. The apples can be cut into very small pieces and mixed in with the batter, if preferred.

NOTES FOR THE TEACHER.

If oyster plants are used instead of parsnips, and are put on to boil as soon as the pupils come, both kinds of fritters can be made. Two bunches of oyster plants and two or three apples will be required. Explain to the class that a drop batter is one which is stiff enough to hold on the surface the drops falling onto it from the mixing spoon. Butter and nicely prepared beef suet are always more wholesome than lard for every purpose, but so many persons use lard that it is given in some of the recipes ; it should always be of the best quality.

Lesson 19.

Uncooked vegetables which are to be used for salads should be most carefully washed and freshened in cold water. They should be pulled apart with the hand and not cut with a knife, unless it is so directed.

Lettuce, water-cresses, celery, raw cabbage, cold boiled string beans, and the green tops of cold asparagus are among those most commonly used for salads.

The cold asparagus tops should be cut into pieces about an inch long and mixed with lettuce leaves. Then sprinkle them with a little powdered sugar, and serve with boiled salad dressing. An underdone cauliflower broken into branches, and mixed with lettuce leaves, is also very nice for a salad. Hard-boiled eggs sliced or cut into small pieces, slices of cold red beets, silver onions, red radishes, and several other vegetables can be used very prettily in various ways for a garnish.

Onions can be sliced with tomatoes or with cucumbers, and dressed with a little pepper, salt, and vinegar. Onion juice is often used as a flavoring, and is obtained by cutting an onion, and pressing the cut side, with a screwing motion, against a grater which should be placed on a saucer so that the juice may run into it.

Cucumbers should be laid in salted water for an hour; then peel and slice them, and put them on ice. They are generally dressed with a little pepper, salt and vinegar.

When used as a garnish, parsley is broken into small sprigs; but when used in cooking, the leaves should be stripped from the stems, and chopped very fine with a knife. Dried herbs should always be rubbed through a fine sieve.

Celery should be laid in very cold water or on ice, as this makes it crisp. When used in salads, it is cut into small dice.

For meat salads, cold chicken, cold veal or ham are used. The meat should always be entirely cold and firm, and it is better to cook it the day before.

The best olive oil should be used for salad dressing, and most dressings should be mixed quickly with a wooden spoon or a silver fork. Boiled salad dressing, and Mayonnaise dressing can be kept for some days in tightly corked bottles, if they are in a cool place.

BOILED SALAD DRESSING.

Put one tablespoonful of sugar, one even tablespoonful of salt, and one teaspoonful of raw mustard in a bowl. Add one tablespoonful of olive oil or melted butter, and mix them together until perfectly smooth. Add three eggs, or four yolks of eggs, and beat well. Then slowly add about two-thirds of a cup of vinegar, and lastly one cupful of milk which has been boiled and cooled somewhat. Pour the mixture into the double boiler, and cook till it thickens, which will be in about five minutes. Stir it while on the fire, and as soon as it begins to thicken take it quickly off, or it will curdle. Set the saucepan into a pan of cold water for a few minutes.

SALAD DRESSING.

Mix together in a deep plate or bowl one saltspoonful of salt, one saltspoonful of dry mustard, and one saltspoonful of pepper, and stir slowly into them with a wooden spoon two tablespoonfuls of olive oil, and lastly one tablespoonful of vinegar. This dressing can be used with lettuce.

POTATO SALAD.

Cut up four or five cold potatoes into small dice, and put them loosely in layers on a dish, sprinkling each layer with a little finely chopped parsley, and pouring a little boiled salad dressing over each with a spoon. Garnish with some sprigs of parsley and slices of potato, which should be laid round the edge of the dish. A small onion can be chopped and mixed with thé potato.

NOTES FOR THE TEACHER.

The pupils will have time to make both the boiled salad dressing and the potato salad, if the potatoes are prepared beforehand and ready for them. All the materials and all the cooking utensils which will be required for a lesson should always be neatly arranged by the teacher, on the table before the pupils come. Flour, sugar, salt and many other things can be kept on hand, and the others can easily be ordered the day before. Time is of great value in a school of cookery, and they will form the habit of preparing everything themselves at home quite as quickly from seeing it regularly done, as they would, if obliged to do it.

CAKES AND DESSERTS.

Lesson 20.

Cake should be made of the best materials, and should be mixed in an earthenware bowl, and with a wooden spoon. A split spoon is good for sponge cake, and a painter's large palette knife is excellent for mixing cake which requires a "cutting in" motion. A small palette knife is better for icing cake than a common knife is. Have all the material ready on the table, then make the cake quickly, mix it lightly and bake it at once in a moderate, steady oven. The pans should be nicely buttered, and for molasses gingerbread and some kinds of cake it is better to line the pan with buttered paper. A piece of white paper can be laid over the top of the cake if it bakes too quickly. If a straw run into the centre of a cake comes out clean, it shows that the cake is done. Most kinds of cake should be taken from the pan at once, and cooled slowly on a sieve turned upside down; but angel cake and a few others are cooled in the pan. If the pans are not papered, the edge and sides of the cake can be loosened carefully with a knife. Stirring butter until it is light and creamy is called "creaming" it. If it is very cold, warm the bowl just enough to soften the butter without melting it. In creaming butter and sugar together, always cream the butter first, and then work in the sugar.

DOVER CAKE.

One pound of unsifted flour, one pound of sugar, half a pound of butter, six eggs, half a pint of milk, one teaspoonful of baking powder, and one nutmeg.

Cream the butter and stir the sugar well into it. Beat the eggs, and add them with the grated nutmeg, and also the milk, stirring constantly as each is added. Lastly sift in the flour with the baking powder in it. If it seems too stiff, add a little more milk. Bake in a pan with a tube in the centre, or in cups. It will require from thirty-five to forty minutes.

Half a pound of citron cut into very small pieces will improve it.

BERWICK SPONGE CAKE.

Beat six eggs two minutes; add three cupfuls of granulated sugar and beat five minutes; sift in two cupfuls of flour with two teaspoonfuls of cream of tartar in it, and beat two minutes; add a cupful of water with one teaspoonful of soda dissolved in it, and beat one minute; add the grated peel and half the juice of a lemon, and sift in two more cupfuls of flour with quarter of a teaspoonful of salt in it. Beat all of these together for another minute, and bake in a deep pan with a tube in the centre, or bake it in a sheet from two to three inches thick, and cut in square pieces. Observe carefully the times of beating.

PLAIN ICING.

Allow one scant cupful of powdered sugar to the white of an egg, but the quantity of sugar should be varied according to the size of the egg. They should be beaten to a stiff paste and spread smoothly over the cake with a small palette knife. A little lemon or orange juice, or a few drops of some extract may be added. Lemon and vanilla can be used together, putting one in the icing and the other in the cake; but almond should never be used in the same cake with lemon or vanilla. Icing will harden better in a cool place.

NOTES FOR THE TEACHER.

The Dover cake and the icing are to be made in this lesson. If the cake is baked in small earthenware baking cups, each pupil will have an opportunity to practice icing. The Berwick cake can be made in some future lesson, or used by the girls in their own homes. It would be well to tell them that angel cakes and a few others are baked in unbuttered pans, and then show them how to beat the whites of the eggs a little before beginning to add the sugar.

Lesson 21.

It is impossible to give recipes which can always be followed exactly in cooking. Flour is affected by a damp atmosphere and varies in weight; different kinds of flour vary also in the amount of water they can absorb; eggs vary in size, and seasonings and flavorings vary in strength; and therefore judgment and experience must always be more or less followed. The dough must be made of the right consistency by the addition of a little more flour or liquid than the recipe may call for; and the soups and sauces should be carefully seasoned, and tested by tasting.

When the oven is to be used, the fire should be cleared, and fresh coal should be put on just as long beforehand as will allow time for the fire to come up and bring the oven to the right heat for baking. Put on coal enough at first to last through the whole time that the oven will be in use; but if it is absolutely necessary to add any, put on a few pieces at a time so as not to chill the fire and the oven. If properly managed, a fire and oven will give no trouble, but no oven will bake well directly after fresh coal has been put on. When the baking is finished, clear the fire again ; put on coal, and close the drafts so as to keep the fire low, until more heat is required. After the fire is kindled in the morning, wood should never be used on a stove or range which is intended for coal. If pieces of wood are put on top of coal, they will deaden the fire, and the heat is only temporary and does much more harm than good.

GOLD CAKE.

Two cupfuls of flour, one cupful of sugar, half a cupful of butter, the yolks of six eggs, one teaspoonful of baking powder, one teaspoonful of orange extract, or a little grated nutmeg.

Cream the butter and sugar, and stir in the beaten yolks, and then the flour sifted a second time with the baking powder in it, beating them all well together. Lastly add the orange extract, and bake in a round pan with a tube in the centre, or in a square baking pan. If the gold and silver cakes are to be used together it is better to bake them in pans of the same shape.

SILVER CAKE.

Half a cupful of butter ; one cupful of powdered sugar ; the whites of six eggs ; half a cupful of milk ; one teaspoonful of baking powder ; two cupfuls of sifted flour, and one teaspoonful of almond extract.

Cream the butter and sugar together, sift the flour again with the baking powder in it, and add the milk and the flour alternately in small quantities to the butter and sugar ; add the beaten whites, stirring rapidly all the time, and astly add the flavoring. Bake about half an hour in a square baking pan so that the cake can be cut into square pieces, or in a long narrow loaf. It should be iced before it is cold.

GINGER SNAPS.

Half a cupful of butter packed tightly; half a cupful of brown sugar; half a pint of molasses (either New Orleans or Porto Rico); one teaspoonful of ginger, half a teaspoonful of cinnamon; half a teaspoonful of soda dissolved in a teaspoonful of boiling water, and one scant quart of unsifted flour.

Cream the butter in a bowl with a wooden spoon; add the sugar, then the molasses, cinnamon and ginger, and the soda in the teaspoonful of boiling water. Sift the flour in gradually, and when it becomes stiff, work the balance in with the hand. Turn onto a well floured bread board; roll very thin, and cut into round cakes with a cutter. Bake a dark brown in a quick oven.

NOTES FOR THE TEACHER.

Let the pupils make the gold and silver cakes, and show them how to mix and bake them nicely and carefully. The ginger snaps are not to be made in this lesson. The batter for the silver cake should be rather stiff, and the whites of the eggs should not be beaten too long as it is apt to cause a little dryness in the consistency of the cake.

Lesson 22.

In every pantry there should be a tin box for cake, one for bread, and a covered jar for the clean pieces of bread. Cake and bread should never be put into a box or shut up until they are entirely cool; and they should always be cooled slowly, for if placed suddenly in a very cold place, or in the strong draft of a door or window, they will be apt to fall a little and be heavy. Pieces of bread can be used for puddings, griddle cakes, and stuffing for meat; and they can also be dried without browning them, in a cool oven, and then crushed and sifted and used for frying oysters, chops and croquettes. These bread crumbs should be kept in a tightly covered glass jar, and it is well to have some always on hand. Never put back into the jar, however, any that have been moistened at all, for they will become musty.

Tin moulds for puddings and other desserts should be kept very clean and bright, or they will blacken whatever is cooked or moulded in them. Pudding cloths should be wrung out in hot water and floured; they should be left loose so as to allow room for the pudding to swell, but the string should be tied around tightly or the water may get in. A pudding should be put into boiling water enough to cover it well, and should not stop boiling even for a moment, as it will make it heavy. Puddings should be cooked as soon as they are mixed (unless otherwise directed), for it hurts them to stand, especially if there is dried fruit in them. Blanc Mange, jellies and ice cream can be taken out easily from the mould, if a cloth wet in hot water is wrapped round it, or the mould can be dipped quickly into hot water.

Dried currants should be carefully picked over and washed, and then dried. Raisins should always be seeded, even if they are to be used whole. Dried fruits should be dredged with flour, when used in cakes or puddings, and should always be the last thing added.

BREAD PUDDING.

Break some stale bread into very small pieces, and put a large half pint of them to soak in a quart of milk for half an hour or longer. Then break three eggs in a bowl and beat them for a minute or two, add three heaping tablespoonfuls of sugar, and stir into them the bread and milk. Butter a pudding dish and pour in the pudding. Divide a tablespoonful of butter into litte bits and put them over the top, and also grate a quarter of a nutmeg over it. Bake in a quick oven from twenty to twenty-five minutes and serve either hot or cold.

A richer pudding can be made by using five eggs, and adding half a cupful of dried currants or seeded raisins. It can be varied also by putting a layer of fruit jelly over the top of the pudding after it is baked and has cooled somewhat, and covering this with a meringue, made with the whites of three of the eggs, and two even tablespoonfuls of powdered sugar. Then put it in the oven a moment to brown.

COLD SAUCE.

Cream half a cupful of butter in a bowl, and stir half a cupful or more of powdered sugar gradually into it (using a wooden spoon or the hand) until it is smooth and stiff and very white. Then add a little grated nutmeg, or lemon juice, or essence of any kind, and pile it up lightly on a small dish. Set it in a cold place, or on ice.

HOT SAUCE.

Take half a pound of butter and half a pound of fine powdered sugar, and beat them to a froth with the hand or a wooden spoon. Then pour on it a large half pint of boiling water, stirring briskly all the time. Have ready on the sauce dish some grated nutmeg or essence of lemon, pour the sauce onto it, and serve at once.

NOTES FOR THE TEACHER.

Let the pupils put the bread in soak as soon as they come, and when the lesson has been given, they can make the bread pudding and the whole quantity of cold sauce which is given in the recipe. Show them how to get the little stems from the currants by rubbing them gently between the hands, or on a sieve.

Lesson 23.

In every kitchen there should be several cloths to be used in boiling meat, fish, and puddings. They should be made of new unbleached cotton, and hemmed and marked. There should also be a bag for straining jelly, several common cloths for taking pans out of the oven, or handling anything hot, and some holders with loops. A piece of zinc is very convenient to stand hot kettles and pans on, and saves the table from a black mark.

Milk, butter, and all materials which are to be used in cooking, should be fresh and sweet, and of the best quality. Care should always be taken also to use exactly the right quantity of everything, as success depends on attention to details, and every part should be rightly and properly done.

When mixing and stirring, be careful to mix in constantly what remains on the sides of the bowl so that the mixture may be smooth and even throughout; and if it is poured or changed from one bowl to another, scrape it all out neatly with a spoon or a small palette knife. Metal spoons will darken anything which has an acid in it, and it is always better to take a spoon out and lay it on a plate when it is not actually in use. It is often impossible to flavor or season a dish rightly without tasting it; this should always be done neatly and nicely by pouring a little from the mixing spoon into another spoon; never taste with the mixing spoon until it has been washed.

Batter should be made just before it is to be used, and should be beaten up very light with an egg-whisk. The yolks or whites of eggs can be kept for one or two days in a cool place, if the bowl is tightly covered with paper. If there is anything in the oven, be careful not to take off the covers of the stove, as it would interfere with the baking. Therefore be a beefsteak if is to broiled for dinner, it is better to select a cold dessert which can be prepared beforehand.

NEW BEDFORD PUDDING.

Four tablespoonfuls of flour, four tablespoonfuls of yellow cornmeal, four eggs, one quart of boiling milk, one cupful of molasses, and one even teaspoonful of salt.

Scald the corn meal with some of the boiling milk, and

stir into it the flour, salt, molasses, and the well beaten eggs. Then slowly add the rest of the milk (which should have been cooled a little) and bake in a well buttered pudding dish, from two to three hours, in a moderate oven. Serve with cold butter, or with sauce.

COTTAGE PUDDING.

Two cupfuls of flour, two eggs, three-quarters of a cupful of sugar, two tablespoonfuls of butter, one cupful of milk, one teaspoonful of baking powder, and half a teaspoonful of salt.

Sift the flour with the baking powder and salt in it, and cream the butter and sugar together in a warm bowl. Beat the eggs until very light, and add them to the butter and sugar; then add the milk, and stir all into the flour very lightly and quickly. Pour the mixture into a buttered pudding dish, and bake to a light brown in a quick oven. Serve with hot lemon sauce.

CUSTARD SAUCE.

One pint of milk, half a cupful of sugar, and the yolks of four eggs. Mix the eggs into the sugar without beating them and add the milk. Set on the fire in a double boiler, and stir until it thickens.

A sponge cake which is not quite fresh can be steamed until very hot; then break it into large pieces, and serve in a dish with this sauce poured over it.

NOTES FOR THE TEACHER.

Let the pupils make the cottage pudding, and half of the quantity of hot sauce given in the recipe in the twenty-second lesson. The other recipes can be used in their own homes.

Lesson 24.

Rice should be picked over carefully, and then thoroughly washed in several waters, rubbing it gently and draining it through a fine strainer. It is used as a vegetable, and also for desserts of various kinds. Cold rice can be made into rice croquettes, and can be used in griddle cakes, corncakes, and waffles. Always soften it first, however, in a little milk, and break up the lumps.

Tapioca and sago are used chiefly in desserts. Sago, and the tapioca which comes in lumps, should be put in soak overnight in milk or water. Pearl tapioca comes in fine grains, and should be used in making tapioca cream; and there is also a finely powdered tapioca which is used for thickening soups.

Sweet apples are sometimes baked whole with the skins on, but should never be cooked in any other way. Greening apples should be used for dumplings, pies, and strained apple sauce; and Spitzenberg and Baldwin apples for apple and tapioca pudding, and for unsweetened, or sweetened apple sauce which is to be left as whole as possible.

APPLE AND TAPIOCA PUDDING.

Put two-thirds of a cupful of tapioca in soak overnight in a pint of cold water. Pour on it the next day one pint of boiling water, and let it stand for an hour or more, stirring it occasionally until it is dissolved. Peel and core six or seven apples and put them in a buttered pudding dish, placing one in the centre and the others in a circle round it. Fill the hole in each with a little sugar, and grated nutmeg or ground cinnamon; pour in the tapioca round them, and bake until the apples are tender and thoroughly cooked, but they should retain their shape. Serve it either hot or cold, with sugar and either cream or milk.

For a late dinner, the tapioca can be put in soak early in the morning. Sago can be used instead of tapioca or a custard can be poured round the apples and baked with them.

GROUND RICE PUDDING.

Three full tablespoonfuls of ground rice, four eggs, one quart of milk, one and a half cupfuls of sugar, a little lemon juice or extract, and a quarter of a teaspoonful of salt.

Mix the ground rice and the salt with a little cold milk, and stir it into a quart of boiling milk; let it boil about fifteen minutes, stirring all the time. When cold, add the beaten eggs, the sugar, and the lemon juice; put it in a buttered pudding dish, and bake it one hour. The dish can be lined with paste if preferred.

SAGO PUDDING.

Put a cupful of sago into a pint of milk, and set it near the fire to swell, stirring it often. When ready for use, add a pint of cold milk, two cups of sugar, a quarter of a teaspoonful of salt, a little grated nutmeg, and five well beaten eggs. Put it in a buttered pudding dish, and bake for an hour and a half in a moderate oven. Tapioca can be used instead of sago.

NOTES FOR THE TEACHER.

Let the pupils make the apple and tapioca pudding, and if there is time, they might make a little apple sauce. It would be well also to question them thoroughly on the previous lessons.

Lesson 25.

If butter is too salt it can be washed in cold water, pressing out all the water with a wooden spoon. Paste may be made with butter, with lard, or with butter and lard together. Lard makes a more tender paste; but it is not so flaky as that which is made with butter. Paste should be made as quickly as possible and in a cold place. If it should work soft, do not keep adding more flour, but put it on ice; or in winter set it in the open air for a time. When it has hardened, work it again. In trimming off the raw paste from the edge of the plate, hold the blade of the knife pointed outward, and cut with a sawing motion. In laying the under crust on the plate, lift it up a little once or twice, and do not stretch it too tightly; the upper crust should always be pricked with a fork in several places. Tin pie plates and graniteware pie plates are considered the best, but the pies should be removed from them as soon as they are baked.

Meat pies can be made from either cooked or uncooked meat; if they are made from cold meat, cut the meat into pieces, add any cold gravy that may be left, some sliced or chopped onion, a little pepper and salt, and enough stock or water to make a gravy; thicken it with a little butter and flour made into a smooth paste as for a roux. If there should be any pie left, it is better to eat it cold; veal pie becomes very unwholesome if heated a second time.

Many persons prefer always to cook the meat somewhat before making a pie, for if raw meat is used, the paste will become hard and dry before the meat has cooked long enough to be tender.

PLAIN PASTE.

One quart of sifted flour, one tablespoonful of butter, three tablespoonfuls of lard, one scant teaspoonful of salt, and half a cupful of ice water, or enough to make a stiff dough.

Rub the lard and salt into the flour with the tips of the fingers, until it is dry and crumbly. Add the water slowly, and mix the dough with a knife. Finally gather it into a lump with the fingers, and turn it onto a board lightly dusted with flour. Flatten it by pounding lightly with the rolling pin, and dot it over with the butter in little bits. Roll it up, and if it can be put in a cold place, or on ice for a time, it will make it more flaky. When ready, roll it about an eighth of an inch thick, and cover the bottom and sides of a pie plate, laying it on a little full and trimming the edge neatly. Then wet it on the edge with a little cold water, and lay round it a narrow strip of paste, pressing them lightly together. Put in the filling, wet the strip with cold water and put on the top crust; prick it with a fork and bake the pie at once.

The top crust can be made richer by taking out enough dough for the bottom crust, before adding the butter.

If more butter is used, it should be divided into several equal parts, and each part should be rolled in separately, using no additional flour.

APPLE PIE.

Five or six apples will make a pie; they should be peeled, cored and cut into very thin slices. After covering the pie plate carefully with the dough for the under paste, fill the dish with the slices of apple, piling them higher in the middle, and sprinkle in with them a heaping cupful of sugar, and a little nutmeg or cinnamon. Then cover them with dough, trimming it neatly, and pricking or scoring it; and bake in a moderate oven. After the top crust is done, let the pie stand for a few minutes in the oven, with the door open.

MOCK APPLE PIE.

Two soda-crackers, one cup of cold water, the grated rind and juice of one lemon, and flour and butter enough to make the paste.

Soak the crackers in the water until it is absorbed, and then add the lemon and the sugar, beating them until smooth and well mixed. Bake in a deep pie plate with both under and upper paste.

SQUASH PIE.

Peel the squash and cut it into pieces; then steam it until very soft, and strain it through a sieve. For every quart of squash add one teaspoonful of salt, two even teaspoonfuls of ginger, half a teaspoonful of cinnamon, one cupful and a half of sugar, and a quart of milk or cream. Mix them well with the squash, and add from two to five well beaten eggs. Bake in deep pie plates lined with paste, and with a thick rim. Cut a rim of paper to cover the crust, if it browns too fast; bake half an hour.

NOTES FOR THE TEACHER.

The whole lesson should be dictated, and then let the pupils make the plain paste and the apple pie; if there is more dough then is required for the pie, they might be shown how to make a turnover. Great care has been taken to make the recipes in these lessons as clear as possible, and to give not only the ingredients, but the best methods of putting them together, so that the pupils can easily cook from them at home. In cooking, it is better to let beginners profit by the experience of others, for it is a waste of their time and brains to oblige them to puzzle over and work out for themselves things which can only be well done by those who have knowledge and judgment. There are many ways in which the mental faculties can be exercised and developed, but in teaching cooking give them everything as clearly and concisely as possible.

BREAKFAST DISHES.

Lesson 26.

Coffee, tea, cocoa and chocolate should be made just before they are to be served, for if they are boiled or steeped too long, they become bitter and injurious. In making coffee and tea, the water should be boiling and also freshly boiled, for water which has been boiling several hours is not fit for such purposes. Coffee-pots and tea-pots should be thoroughly washed and dried whenever they are used. Tea should be made in an earthenware tea-pot, and never in one made of tin; if a silver or plated tea-pot is used, stand it always on the table and not on or near the stove, for heat will melt silver. Both coffee and tea should be kept in tightly covered canisters.

Most grocers keep roasted coffee on hand, but it should be bought in small quantities and unground, for coffee will lose its flavor if it is not used as soon as it is ground. If coffee is to be roasted at home it should be put in a pan into a moderately hot oven and constantly stirred with a wooden spoon, or coffee stick until it is all of an even brown color. The best coffee is made from Java and Mocha coffees mixed in the proportion of one-third Mocha to two-thirds Java. Many persons prefer drip coffee, which is made by filtering boiling water slowly through finely ground coffee, and patented coffee-pots on this principal can be bought at the house-furnishing stores.

COFFEE.

Allow one heaping tablespoonful of coffee, and half an egg-shell to every cupful of water. After scalding the coffee-pot, break up the egg-shells and put them in, then add the coffee and cold water enough to moisten it, and lastly pour on the boiling water. Cover tightly and let it boil gently about four minutes; pour out a cupful to clear the spout from grounds and return it to the coffee-pot, and let it stand at the back of the stove a few minutes to settle. Serve in the same coffee-pot if possible, as it loses flavor if poured into another.

For strong black coffee, a larger quantity of ground coffee must be used with the same quantity of water.

TEA.

Allow one full teaspoonful of tea for each person, and an extra one to make good strength. Scald the tea-pot; put in the dry tea-leaves and pour on them a small quantity of boiling water. Let the tea-pot stand on the table for a minute or two, and then pour on as much more boiling water as is required.

In making English breakfast tea, it is better to pour on all the boiling water at once.

MILK TOAST.

Put one pint of milk on the fire in a double boiler. Warm a tablespoonful of butter and stir smoothly into it one tablespoonful of flour, adding a saltspoonful of salt, and a tablespoonful of the warm milk. When the rest of the milk boils, add the mixture slowly to it, stirring constantly until it thickens, and then set it at the back of the stove. Toast five or six slices of baker's bread and butter them while hot. Then dip each into the thickened milk long enough to soften it, and put it in a hot dish. When all are dipped, pour the milk over them and serve at once.

CORN CAKE.

Sift together one cup of yellow or white cornmeal, one cup of flour, two even teaspoonfuls of baking powder, and half a teaspoonful of salt, and add one quarter of a cup of sugar. Beat well one or two eggs, and stir into them one cup of milk; then melt quickly one large tablespoonful of butter in a small saucepan or tin cup, and add it to the milk and eggs and mix them at once into the flour and cornmeal before the butter has time to cool. Bake in deep layer cake pans, or any shallow pan, filling them only half full. A quick oven is required.

NOTES FOR THE TEACHER.

Let the pupils make the corn cake and the coffee, leaving the other recipes to be used at home. It would be well to tell them something about the various effects produced on different persons by coffee and tea; and that when taken in moderation, they are often beneficial, while they become very injurious if taken to excess either in strength or quantity. Ask them also something about cornmeal, oatmeal and the different grains.

Lesson 27.

Sugar, salt, soda, cream of tartar and all powders should be carefully freed from lumps by crushing or pounding them, and by sifting them through a fine sieve. One teaspoonful of soda and two teaspoonfuls of cream of tartar is the proportion for one quart of flour, and the directions for using them are generally given in the recipes in which they occur. If soda is used with sour milk, put just enough soda into the sour milk to sweeten it. Usually it is dissolved in a little hot water, and when pouring it into the dough or batter be careful to leave in the cup the little coarse grains which have settled in the bottom of it. One heaping teaspoonful of baking powder will raise one pint of flour, and it is better to sift the salt and the baking powder with the flour. When soda, cream of tartar, or baking powder are used, the dough or batter should be lightly and quickly mixed and cooked at once. Some persons prefer to beat batter and others prefer to stir it; the first method will make cake porous; but the last will make it more tender and velvety. In putting ingredients together, flour and milk should always be added very slowly. Flour is sometimes sprinkled or sifted into the other ingredients, and sometimes it is better to add them slowly to the flour. If a small quantity of flour is used for thickening, it should be mixed into a smooth paste with a little milk, water, or melted butter, and then slowly stirred into the hot liquid. For gravies and sauces, butter is generally used as it will make them richer. If butter is melted over too hot a fire or is left too long on the stove, it will become oily; it should merely be heated until soft enough to mix easily with the flour, or sugar. In cold weather it is sometimes impossible to cream butter without warming it a little. This can be done by setting the bowl on the tea-kettle until the steam has softened the butter, without melting it at all.

COCOA.

For one quart of cocoa, take one pint of milk, one pint of water and three tablespoonfuls of cocoa. Put the water and milk in a saucepan on the fire, and mix the cocoa with enough hot water to make a smooth paste. When the milk is boiling, stir the cocoa slowly into it; let it boil a few minutes, and serve in a cocoa-pot which has been scalded. Half a cupful of sugar can be added, if desired; but as some persons prefer it unsweetened, it is better to sweeten it at the table, so as to suit the different tastes.

OATMEAL.

There are several different kinds of oatmeal, which are of different grades of fineness, and some of them require to be cooked longer than others. Steamed oatmeal which comes in packages can be cooked in half an hour, and for unsteamed oatmeal these directions can be followed.

Put one quart of water into a double boiler, and when it boils add one teaspoonful of salt, and one cupful of oatmeal, stirring it slowly in. Let it boil then at least two hours without stirring it at all and fill up the under saucepan with boiling water as often as is necessary to keep it from drying entirely away.

GRAHAM BISCUIT.

Three even cups of graham flour, one even cup of white flour, one teaspoonful of salt, two teaspoonfuls of baking powder, one pint of milk, two tablespoonfuls of butter, and one or two eggs.

Sift the graham flour, the white flour, the salt and the baking powder together in a bowl. Break the egg into a small bowl, beat it well, and stir the milk slowly into it. Melt the butter and add it while hot to the milk and egg; then stir them into the flour and meal, and beat them about five minutes. Butter the gem-pans and fill them about two-thirds full; then bake in a quick oven twenty minutes.

NOTES FOR THE TEACHER.

Let the pupils make the cocoa, and the graham biscuit, and boil a little steamed oatmeal; and tell them how wholesome graham meal is, and how much better it is to use it part of the time, instead of using nothing but white flour.

Lesson 28.

"A place for everything and everything in its place" should be the motto for every kitchen, pantry and closet. There should be tight wooden buckets for flour, corn-meal, rice and sugar, and covered glass or stone jars, and wooden or tin boxes for the other materials which are kept on hand. Cornstarch, oatmeal and other things which come in packages should be put into boxes or jars, and not left loose in the paper and exposed to the dust. There should also be two bowls with lips, kept expressly for milk and used alternately; a wooden salt-box with a hinged cover, as salt should never be kept in tin; a "Foster" patent flour safe and sifter, which is much better for holding flour than a wooden bucket is; two dredging boxes of different colors, one for flour and one for powdered sugar; old cloths to wipe the floor and shelves, a tin match-box, a knife-board, a towel roller, and kettles, pans, saucepans and enough other cooking utensils to do the work comfortably and properly. Each one of these should be kept thoroughly clean and dry and in its own place. Sapolio is excellent for cleaning tin or wooden ware, and a little soda will clean iron kettles which have been neglected. If bread-pans, baking-pans and waffle irons are not kept very clean, especially in the corners, they will leave a black mark on everything which is cooked in them, and the crust of the bread will soon have an unpleasant taste. Copper cooking utensils require especial care, and should be kept perfectly clean and bright, as the green rust which forms on them is poisonous. Bread and cake boxes should be frequently aired at the window, or in the sun, and refrigerators should be wiped out, and kept sweet and dry and closely shut, except when open for a time to air them.

BOILED EGGS.

Lay the eggs in warm water for a minute to prevent the shells from cracking; then drop them gently into fast boiling water. Allow three minutes for a soft boiled egg, four minutes if the white is to be set firmly, and ten minutes for what is commonly called a hard boiled egg. It is much better, however, to boil eggs for about thirty minutes if we wish them to be really hard boiled. They will then be thoroughly cooked, and digestible.

BREAD GRIDDLE CAKES.

Pour one pint of hot scalded milk onto one pint of breadcrumbs, and stir into them one full tablespoonful of butter. Let them soak all night and then rub them through a vegetable strainer, and add two beaten eggs. Sift together one even cupful of flour, one-half teaspoonful of salt, and two teaspoonfuls of baking powder, and mix them slowly with the crumbs, adding if necessary a little cold milk. Bake in small round cakes on the griddle, and serve hot.

WAFFLES.

One even pint of flour, three eggs, one and a quarter cupfuls of milk, one tablespoonful of butter, half a teaspoonful of salt, and one teaspoonful of baking powder.

Sift the flour, the salt and the baking powder together into a bowl. Beat the eggs and add the milk slowly to them; then melt the butter and add it, and stir the mixture into the flour until the batter is smooth. Beat it up lightly for a few minutes with an egg-whisk, and bake in a waffle-iron, filling it about half full. Serve the waffles hot, with a little powdered sugar sifted or dredged over each one.

The waffle-iron should be well heated and buttered before the batter is put in, and also between each set of waffles. Let the batter always get somewhat firm and stiff, before turning the waffle-iron over; otherwise it will run out, and the waffles will be thin and heavy.

NOTES FOR THE TEACHER.

Let the pupils make the waffles, and some tea according to the recipe given in the twenty-sixth lesson. It would be well to show them how to mix batter carefully and nicely, and how to manage a waffle-iron. Let each pupil in turn bake a waffle.

Lesson 29.

The small knives which come for paring vegetables are very useful in a kitchen, and there should be also a sharp meat knife, a bread knife, a large palette knife for mixing cake, and one or two small palette knives. A wooden knife is useful for many purposes, and there should be several wooden spoons, and plenty of bowls of all sizes, and a coffee cup for measuring sugar and butter. A coffee cup holds about half a pint, and a half pint measure can be used instead of it. There is a brown glazed earthenware which is used for jars and cooking utensils, and is very good for boiling rice, potatoes and other vegetables, but it should never be used for fruit or for anything acid, because acids act on some kinds of glazing just as they do on tin or zinc, and may become poisonous. Neither vinegar nor even sweet milk should be put in them, for the milk might sour. It is best to be careful also in measuring and mixing anything which is acid; extracts, and the juice of fruits should be measured in china spoons or glass measuring cups, and not in iron or leaden spoons, and bowls are much better for mixing purposes than tin pans are. Care should be taken never to put anything hot or even warm into a refrigerator, as the sudden change will affect it injuriously. Milk and butter are often affected by fruits and vegetables in the same refrigerator, and should be kept separate from them.

CHOCOLATE.

Two squares of baker's, or any unsweetened chocolate, half a cupful of sugar, one pint of milk, and one pint of water, one teaspoonful of cornstarch.

Put the milk and water on the fire in a double boiler; then grate or scrape the chocolate very fine and put it in a saucepan with a tablespoonful of hot water. Stir it for a few minutes on the fire until it is smooth and glossy, and when the milk and water are boiling, pour them slowly into it, stirring all the time. Let all boil for a minute, and then stir into it one teaspoonful of cornstarch or arrowroot made into a smooth paste with a little cold water. Boil for about a minute and serve.

A little thick whipped cream either sweetened or unsweetened can be served on the top of each cup.

SALLY LUNN.

One pint of flour, two tablespoonfuls of sugar, half a teaspoonful of salt, two eggs, half a cupful of butter, half a cupful of milk, and two teaspoonfuls of baking powder.

Sift together the flour, the sugar, the salt, and the baking powder. Beat the eggs and add the milk slowly to them, then add the butter after melting it and stir the mixture at once into the flour, beating them all up lightly. Bake fifteen minutes in a large round pan with a tube in the centre, or in gem pans, and dredge a little powdered sugar over the top before serving.

Very nice gem cakes can be made for breakfast by this recipe with the sugar omitted.

SHORT-CAKE.

One quart of flour, one cup of butter, half a pint of milk, and one teaspoonful of salt.

Sift together the flour, the salt, and the baking powder; rub in the butter; heat the milk and add it slowly. After mixing the dough, roll it out lightly, and cut into small squares, and bake a light brown in a quick oven.

This same dough can be baked in deep layer cake pans and used for strawberry short-cake.

CORNMEAL MUSH.

Put one quart of water in a saucepan on the fire, and when it boils add one even tablespoonful of salt, and take off the little scum from the top; then sprinkle slowly into it with the left hand some yellow or white cornmeal, stirring constantly with a wooden spoon in the right hand. Continue this until the mush is stiff enough, and then let it cook gently for about fifteen or twenty minutes, stirring occasionally; when it is done, it will puff up and bubble. Serve with sugar and milk, or with syrup.

It there is any left over, mould it in a deep square pudding dish and slice and cook it for breakfast the next morning in a frying pan.

NOTES FOR THE TEACHER.

Let the pupils make the Sally Lunn, and boil a little cornmeal mush. Tell them also that whenever they have not quite as much milk as is given in a recipe, it will do no harm to use a little water with it. There is a mistaken impression that the more milk and butter there is in anything, the nicer it will be; whereas too much milk or too much butter will make a thing very heavy. If in trying a recipe for the first time the batter or dough proves to be too soft, it is better to take less milk or water the next time instead of adding more flour.

MISCELLANEOUS DISHES.

Lesson 30.

Fish should be selected with great care, as they are unwholesome if not fresh. Fish when fresh have full clear eyes, bright red gills, and firm flesh. They should be kept in a cold place, and thoroughly cleaned and washed, and carefully dried before they are cooked. They may be boiled, baked, fried, broiled, or made into chowder. The largest fish are generally boiled, the medium sized ones can be either boiled or baked, and the smallest ones are usually fried or broiled. A kettle with a strainer should be used for boiling fish. If there is any cold fish left over, it can be freed from bones, and minced with a little cold potato, a small piece of butter, a little salt and pepper, and a little milk, and then shaped into round cakes and cooked in hot butter in the frying-pan for breakfast, or it can be put into a shallow dish and browned in the oven. Salt mackerel should be put in soak over night, and may be boiled or fried; in the latter case, they should be well dried before cooking them.

BOILED FISH.

Salmon should never be soaked in water, but should be well washed and a little salt should be rubbed into it. Then wrap it in a floured cloth closely fastened, and put it into slightly salted boiling water, allowing five minutes to a pound after it begins to boil. When it is done, take it out, unwrap the cloth carefully, and serve with rich drawn butter with a little minced parsley and lemon juice stirred into it; pouring some of it over the fish. The middle slice of a salmon is considered the best piece to boil.

The head and shoulders of a cod is considered the best part to boil. Lay it in cold salted water for an hour, then scrape and wash it clean, rub in a little salt and cayenne pepper, and wrap it in a floured cloth, fastening it tightly enough to keep all water out, and put it into boiling water, letting it boil gently and allowing four or five minutes to the pound. Then take it out and remove the cloth carefully, taking care not to break the fish, and not to let any water get into the dish. Small fish are boiled whole Egg sauce is generally served with boiled fish. This is drawn butter with small pieces of hard-boiled egg in it, and some of it should always be poured over the fish.

A little vinegar is sometimes put into the water in which fish is boiled, but is never used with salmon.

FRIED FISH.

The fish should be nicely cleaned and washed, and wiped quite dry. Small fish can be dipped in egg and crumbs and fried in a kittle of boiling fat, or they can be dipped in flour or cornmeal and cooked in a frying pan with a little lard or salt pork. In cooking a moderate sized fish in this way, the skin should be slightly scored, and the opening which was made in order to clean the fish, should be fastened over with a small skewer. Small and medium sized fish can be fried whole.

Large fish should be cleaned, boned, and cut into pieces about three or four inches square; these should be washed and wiped dry and can be dipped in egg and crumbs and fried in boiling fat, or cooked in a frying-pan. Fresh cod can be cooked very nicely, by frying some thin slices of fat salt pork in a flat bottomed kettle or deep pan, and when they are brown and crisp take them out on a hot plate, and add enough lard to the melted pork, to cover the fish well. Dip the pieces of fish in egg and either crumbs or flour, and when the fat is boiling hot again, put them in and fry a light brown. Serve with the slices of pork round the edge of the dish, and garnish with sprigs of parsley.

BROILED SHAD.

Scrape and scale a shad, split it down the back, wash it clean and wipe it dry. Lay it in a well-greased fish broiler, and hold the skin side first to the fire. Cook it from ten to twenty minutes according to the size, turning it occasionally. When done, place it on a hot dish, sprinkle it with salt and pepper, and butter it. Large fish require a slower fire than small ones do.

NOTES FOR THE TEACHER.

Let the pupils clean a small fish and cook it in a frying pan, showing them how to prepare it nicely, and how to cook it slowly so that it may get thoroughly done without browning too much. Let them also make the short-cake which was given in the twenty-ninth lesson, showing them how to knead and cut dough without leaving any little pieces of it on the bread-board, for if they are not gathered in each time with the dough, they become dry and hard, and must then be thrown away as they would injure the bread.

Lesson 31.

Poultry should have bright full eyes, and soft moist skin and should be plump and healthy looking. They should be killed by quickly cutting off the head, and not by wringing the neck. Then hang them up for a time with the neck down; pick them and draw them as soon as possible, but do not cook them for at least eight or ten hours after they have been killed.

In buying those which have already been killed, select those which are plump and have fine grained flesh; if turkeys and chickens are tender, the tip of the breast-bone will be tender, and the wing will separate easily if gently pulled. Many persons think that those with light colored skins are nicer and more delicate than those which have deep yellow skins, but every one should follow her own taste in such a matter. If a turkey or chicken is to be boned, care should be taken to buy one which has not been scalded, as that makes the skin very weak.

STUFFING.

Allow a one-pound loaf of baker's bread for an eight or ten pound turkey. Cut off the crust and break the inside into pieces; put these in a bowl, and pour on them water which has been slightly warmed (as very warm water will make them heavy). Let them stand about a minute, and then take up a handful at a time, squeeze it hard with both hands, and place it in a dish until all are done. Toss it lightly with the fingers, and add one teaspoonful of salt, one teaspoonful of pepper, one scant teaspoonful of powdered summer savory, one scant teaspoonful of powdered sage, and lastly a tablespoonful of butter. Work it all thoroughly together, and it can be used for fish and meat as well as for fowls. It can also be varied in many ways by adding other ingredients; some persons add a beaten egg, and for geese and ducks, a little onion chopped fine is used. Chopped parsley and a little chopped salt pork are used in stuffing for fish, and the dried herbs can be omitted. The quantity of stuffing that should be made depends of course on the size of the bird or fish.

BROILED CHICKEN.

After dressing and washing the chicken, split it open through the back bone, cut the cords under the wings, and lay the wings out flat; cut the sinews under the second joint of the leg, and turn the leg down, pressing down the breast bone without breaking it. Rub a little salt over it, and place it on a gridiron over a slow fire, turning the inside first to the fire, and placing a tin sheet and a weight over the chicken to keep it flat. Let it broil eight or ten minutes, and then turn it and cook the other side in the same way, continuing this until the chicken is done. Serve on a hot platter, sprinkling both sides with pepper and putting some small pieces of butter on the upper side.

A broiled chicken should be thoroughly cooked, without being scorched, and in order to insure this, it must be closely watched, and the heat should be distributed as equally as possible.

NOTES FOR THE TEACHER.

Let the pupils clean and broil a chicken, and impress upon them the importance of doing it always thoroughly and carefully. In schools of cookery it is very much better to let the pupils do the work themselves in turn, with what explanation and help may be required from the teacher to enable them to do it rightly. They take more interest and learn much more than they do when one of them does the work and the others look on, and with system and good management this can easily de done.

Lesson 32.

In preparing poultry for cooking, remove all the feathers, singe the bird over a burning newspaper on the top of the stove, take out all the pin feathers, and then draw it very nicely, being careful not to break the gall-bag or any of the other organs. Cut off the head, neck and feet, take out with the finger anything that is in the neck, and wash the inside thoroughly in several waters. Then dry it carefully inside and out with a clean cloth, and fasten the neck close to the body by drawing a piece of skin over it and holding it with a stitch or a small skewer. The gizzard, liver, neck and heart should be cleaned and laid in cold water. Many persons put a little soda in the last water but one with which the inside of a chicken is washed, as it will prevent the bitter taste which is often noticed in the stuffing if a chicken or turkey is not entirely fresh. Poultry which are bought in market should be cleaned and rubbed with a little salt on the inside as soon as they are brought home, even if they are not to be cooked at once. White mending cotton is very good for sewing up fish, birds, and meat because it is softer than thread and does not tear the skin.

ROAST TURKEY.

After preparing the turkey, fill it with stuffing and sew it up; tie or skewer the wings down to the sides, and tie down the legs also unless the butcher has left a strap of skin to hold them. Rub it over with butter, place it evenly on a rack fitted into a dripping pan, pour a little water into the pan, and then sprinkle the turkey with pepper and salt, and dredge it with flour, and put it into the oven. Melt a tablespoonful of butter in a cupful of boiling water, and baste frequently with it; sprinkle the turkey once more with pepper and salt, and dredge it for the last time about fifteen minutes before it is to be taken from the oven. After removing the skewers and strings, serve it on a hot platter, with the gizzard, and garnish with parsley. Cranberry sauce should be served with it.

GRAVY FOR ROAST TURKEY.

Before the turkey is put into the oven to roast, put the neck, heart, liver, and gizzard into a saucepan with a pint and a half of cold water and half a teaspoonful of salt; let them boil gently until they are quite tender, then take them out of the water, leaving that in the saucepan; throw away the neck, leave the gizzard whole to be served with the turkey, and braid the liver and heart fine with a knife, or put them through a sieve. Work into them a small piece of butter and a little flour, and put them back into the water in the saucepan with a quarter of a teaspoonful of pepper. Let the gravy boil gently and stir constantly until it is smooth, and then serve it.

Some persons prefer to remove all fat from the drippings in the pan in which the turkey has been cooked, and to stir this into them and let it all boil a few minutes, and then serve it.

NOTES FOR THE TEACHER.

Let the pupils prepare a small turkey or chicken and put it in the oven before the lesson is given, using the recipe for stuffing which is given in the thirty-first lesson, and making of course a smaller quantity of it. Show them particularly how to prepare the liver for the gravy. If they all stand round a long table, each one can always have a share in the work by letting the girl who stands at the left of the teacher do her part first, and then move round to the right of the teacher.

Lesson 33.

Hams, tongues, and corned beef should be put on in cold water enough to cover them well, and should never be allowed to boil very hard as it will make them tough. When they have boiled for a few minutes at the front of the stove, set them where they will boil gently. The brisket and the aitch-bone are the best pieces of corned beef for boiling, and if bought already corned at the market they will not require to be soaked, but should be cleaned nicely. Boil the beef until tender, allowing about twenty minutes or half an hour to a pound. If it is to be served hot, a cabbage is often cooked with it, and after pressing out carefully all the water, it may be put round the corned beef on the same platter, or served in a separate dish. If the meat is to be served cold, remove the bones, place it in a dish, and put a plate on it with the upper side down, then put a flat-iron on this and leave it until the beef is cold and well pressed. Some persons prefer to let salt meats partly cool in the water in which they have been boiled.

If ham is to be broiled or fried, cut it into slices about a quarter of an inch thick, and trim off carefully the black rim of skin from each slice. If it is very salt, lay it in cold water for half an hour, but dry it well before cooking it. When broiled, or fried, ham and bacon should always be served at one, as they become tough and dry if kept standing by the fire.

A smoked tongue should be washed and put in soak over night; in the morning put it on the stove in cold water, and boil gently until tender, which will take from three to four hours, according to the size. Then take it out, peel off the skin, and serve it cold.

BOILED HAM.

Wash off the dust from the ham and put it in soak over night; in the morning scrape it and put it on the fire in cold water enough to cover it well. Boil it gently for several hours, or until quite tender. Let it partly cool in the water in which it has been boiled, then take it out, remove the skin carefully, and set the ham on a rack in a dripping pan. Sprinkle it well with fine bread crumbs, and let it brown in the oven for a few minutes.

A cold ham bone can always be used in making split pea soup, and will make the soup very nice if it is boiled in it.

DEVILED HAM.

Take the meat which is left of a cold ham, remove the hard dark bits, but leave some fat. Chop it very finely until it is almost a paste; and for a pint of this make the following dressing: mix together one scant teaspoonful of ground mustard, one tablespoonful of sugar, one-quarter of a teaspoonful of Cayenne pepper, and then slowly add two-thirds of a cupful of good vinegar. Stir this into the minced ham, pack it into a mould, and keep in a cool place. Turn it onto a platter, garnish it with parsley, and serve at lunch or breakfast. The roots of a tongue can be used in the same way.

NOTES FOR THE TEACHER.

Buy some cold cooked ham at a restaurant, and if the pupils devil it as soon as they come, it can be turned out and eaten before they leave. They can also fry a slice of raw ham and two or three eggs. The teacher should always remember to question the class on the previous lesson, and occasionally should question them on all the past lessons in turn. Their minds can be developed, and the important facts and principles can be more clearly and strongly impressed upon them by questioning than they can in any other way. It is better also not to give them too much general information, or tell them several different ways of cooking a dish, because it confuses their minds, and if they first learn one method thoroughly, they can easily vary it for themselves after a little experience. Any girl who can answer intelligently and correctly all the questions which are given at the end of these lessons will have a good knowledge of cookery, and will be able to acquire for herself from books and recipes any additional information which she may need, unless she wishes to cook something very difficult and elaborate.

Lesson 34.

On account of the infinite variety which exists in the constitutions and temperaments of different persons, there cannot be any fixed rules given in regard to food; and opinions and theories as to what is best will always vary. Good and well-cooked food is undoubtedly conducive to good health, but it should be adapted to the taste and customs of those who are to eat it. One person may prefer tender, moist bread, and rare meat, while another likes meat well done, and dry, fine-grained bread; and both are equally wholesome. One person will say that beef-tea is not as nourishing as it has been supposed to be, while another, who has seen many lives saved by it, will never accept that theory. The hygiene, chemistry and physiology which you study at school are very interesting, and have a certain relation to what we eat, but cookery is a distinct art by itself, and the best cooks have often known nothing of the laws of health, nor why yeast will cause dough to rise; and therefore in receiving and in practising your cooking lessons you must pay close attention to the facts and principles of *practical* cookery. As the dishes you have made have been intended chiefly for those who are in good health, I will give you in this last lesson a few recipes for dishes which can be used for the sick, and will begin with some general directions in regard to the use of beef-tea.

Beef-essence is very strong, and should be used carefully,

and only for those who are unable to take any other nourishment. A teaspoonful is all that should be given at a time. A half teaspoonful of it given every hour will sometimes bring up a very sick person when nothing else will. It can be used either hot or cold, as the patient may fancy.

Beef-tea is weaker than beef-essence, and when it is given to a very sick person who is taking no food, one ounce every hour, two ounces every two hours, or three ounces every three hours, according to the condition of the patient, has been found to be a very good rule. When it is given merely to strengthen a convalescent, a cupful between meals is sufficient.

It is important to continue to give nourishment through the night to sick persons who are awake, but they should not be wakened for it. Even convalescents will feel stronger in the morning if they have had a cupful of beef-tea or milk in the night.

BEEF-ESSENCE.

Take one pound of the round of beef and cut it into small pieces with a sharp knife, removing every particle of fat, then put in a wide-mouthed bottle, cork it tightly, place it in a kettle of cold water and bring it gradually to a boil. Let it boil three or four hours, and then pour off the juice (which will be about a cupful), and season it with a little salt.

BEEF-TEA NO. 1.

Take one pound of lean beef, and cut it with a sharp knife into small pieces, removing every particle of fat; put it into a bowl with one pint of cold water, and let it soak several hours. Then put the meat and the same water into a covered saucepan and let it gradually come to a boil;

when it has boiled five or six minutes strain it and season it with a little salt and pepper.

BEEF-TEA NO. 2.

Prepare a pound of beef as before, and put it in a kettle with a quart of cold water. Let it boil down one-half, and then strain it, and season with salt and pepper.

The meat for beef-tea should always be cut with a sharp knife drawn quickly through the pieces, leaving them with open edges so that the juice may come out freely. Beef for tea should never be chopped with a chopping knife as it will become a tangled mass from which only a little juice can come, and a part of it will be lost in the wooden tray.

MILK PORRIDGE.

Put one pint of milk on the stove in a double boiler, and mix one even tablespoonful of sifted flour into a smooth paste with a little cold water or milk. When the milk boils, add this slowly to it with a little salt, stirring constantly. Let it boil about five minutes and it is ready for use.

CORNMEAL GRUEL.

Mix one tablespoonful of fine cornmeal with one-half a saltspoonful of salt, and enough cold water to make a smooth paste. Add it slowly to a pint of boiling water, and cook it about twenty minutes, stirring constantly.

This gruel can be made with half a pint of water and half a pint of milk.

OATMEAL GRUEL.

Put four tablespoonfuls of the coarsely ground oatmeal with a little salt into a pint of boiling water. Let it boil gently, and stir constantly until it is as thick as you wish it; then strain it and flavor it with a little nutmeg or anything which is allowed.

NOTES FOR THE TEACHER.

In this lesson the pupils will not be able to make the beef-tea, unless they make one-half of the quantity given in recipe No. 1, and put the beef in soak as soon as they come. It can be soaked for an hour or so and cooked longer than the time which is given, and they will then see how it ought to look, and how it should be cut up. They might make one of the gruels or the porridge, as the teacher may prefer. As this course of lessons is intended to include all that is required to enable girls to understand the different processes of cooking, and to carry it on farther by themselves without more instruction, some of the lessons are unavoidably a little longer than others are. There may also be more lessons than can be given in a limited school year, which is more or less interrupted by holidays; in that case the two lessons on poultry can be omitted, or the last lessons can be hurried by giving a little extra dictation on one day, and a little extra cooking on the next one. Without giving too much time to little unnecessary details, a teacher should have her pupils always under control, and should have the class-room and everything in it kept clean and in good order, and see that the dishes, boxes and brushes are all put back just where they came from, and that everything which contains material is labelled in order to prevent mistakes, which might be dangerous. If she will carry out faithfully and with interest her part of the work, I think that at the end of the year her pupils will show that they have accomplished their's.

QUESTIONS.

ON THE

MANAGEMENT OF A STOVE AND OF A FIRE.

How do you prepare the stove before making a fire in it?
How should the dampers and drafts be arranged?
Where do you put the ashes, and what must be done to them?
When is the best time to put cinders on the fire?
How should the paper and wood be placed?
Is all the coal put on at once?
After the fire is lighted, how do you arrange the dampers?
Why should the upper main damper always be left a little open?
How high should a grate be filled with coal?
If the grate is too full, how does it affect the heat?
What must be done to the fire as soon as the breakfast is entirely cooked?
If there is bread to be baked, how do you prepare the oven?
If there is no more cooking to be done until dinner, what kind of fire do you need?
How does an open door or window opposite a stove affect a fire?
Can you light a fire in winter if the water pipes are frozen?
Is it ever safe to use coal oil in lighting a fire?
What wood is best for kindling?
Which kind of coal is best for a stove, and which for a range?

Are all stoves and ranges managed in the same way?
What kind of fire is needed for baking?
How do you test the oven?
How often should the stove be blacked; and how is it done?
How often should the oven flue be cleaned out?
Are there other flues which require to be cleared?

MANAGEMENT OF BREAD AND BISCUIT.

What are the two kinds of white flour called?
Which should be used for cake or pastry, and which should be used for bread?
Which is the cheapest flour in the end, and where should flour be kept?
If the bread is to be moist and tender, what kind of dough do you make?
How long should it be kneaded?
How should the dough be mixed and kneaded for fine-grained, dry bread?
How should the dough for tip-top biscuit be mixed and kneaded?
How do you knead dough on a bread board, and with what kind of motion?
If too much flour is used, or worked in on the bread board, how does it affect the bread, cake, or pastry?
Why should you cut as many biscuit as possible from each rolling of the dough?
Should bread dough be mixed with cold, or lukewarm water?
Should it be put in a cold or a warm place to rise?
Should bread be treated in winter in the same way as in summer?

How do you cover the pan in which it is set to rise?

What shall you do to the dough in the morning?

How long should bread rise in the pans, and how long should rolls?

Can the rising of dough be hastened in any way?

Should the oven be hotter for rolls than for bread?

What can you tell me about yeast?

How much baker's yeast is required for two quarts of flour?

Will one-third of a cake of Fleischman's yeast raise two quarts of flour?

How can the rest of the cake be kept good for a short time?

Do you make a stiff dough for sugar cookies?

What can you tell me about rolling, cutting, and baking them?

ON BOILING AND THE MANAGEMENT OF BOILED DISHES.

How can you tell when the water in a kettle is boiling?

Where do the bubbles remain when water is only simmering?

Do you put into a saucepan at once all the water which will be needed?

If it boils away too much, should the water that is added be actually boiling?

Should you ever allow anything to stop boiling?

If it should stop even for a minute, what would the effect be?

If you are boiling meat, or vegetables, or puddings, do you let them boil fast?

What effect does gentle boiling have on them?

Is not gentle boiling better for everything?

MANUAL OF COOKERY.

Should saucepans and kettles be filled entirely full?
Why should not they be filled full?
Do you ever leave them on the fire without any water in them?
How would it injure them?
When you put anything on to boil, do you not generally merely cover it well with water?
If you are intending to boil one thing four hours, and another only two hours, would you put the same amount of water with both?
When you are cooking oatmeal, custard, milk, or anything which will burn easily, what kind of boiler do you use?
What is a double boiler?
What can be used in place of it?
Do you fill the lower saucepan with boiling water before putting anything into the upper one?
How can you tell when milk is boiling in a double boiler?
In what other way can potatoes, oatmeal and many other things be cooked?
How often do you wash the tea-kettle, and fill it with fresh water?
Will it injure the tea and coffee if it is not kept clean?
Should you ever use the water from a range boiler for cooking?
How do you prepare the meat and bone for soup stock?
What kind of kettle is it made in.
How much water do you allow for every pound of meat?
How much salt, and how much pepper do you put in for this quantity?
Do you let the meat stand in the water before putting it on the fire?

After putting it on the fire, do you let it come to a boil slowly or fast?

After skimming it why do you still let it boil steadily and gently?

How much time is allowed for every pound of meat?

Should the stock be boiled down much?

When it is done what proportion will it bear to the original quantity of water?

If it does not boil down fast enough what can you do to hasten it?

Do you strain stock?

What do you put it into; and what will form on the top?

Do you remove this cake of fat?

If the stock is made of beef only, what can this fat be used for?

What will the consistency of the stock be in winter?

Can it be used even if it should not become a jelly?

Do you always use the stock for soup without diluting it?

If it is diluted what proportion of water is used?

What is brown stock made from?

What is white stock made from?

What is a stock-pot, and how often should it be emptied and cleaned?

What else do you make soup from; cannot you use cold meat bones?

What do you ask for at the butcher's when you wish to buy meat for soup?

Why must the bones be cracked when they are used for soup?

Can you mention some of the vegetables which are used in soup?

Do you strain a vegetable soup or not?

Do you peel potatoes when you intend to boil them?

Are old and new potatoes treated in the same way?

Should potatoes be put in soak, and should they be put on the fire in boiling or in cold water?

How much salt is allowed to a quart of water in cooking them?

How long do you cook potatoes?

If they are not all of the same size, what can you do?

How do you make them mealy?

How do you mash potatoes?

How do you make what is called potato snow?

In making drawn butter, how do you put the butter and flour together?

How long must you stir the flour into the melted butter?

What do you add then?

How can you make drawn butter more or less rich?

What kinds of meal are used in Boston brown bread?

Do you use any white flour?

Is it made with sweet or sour milk?

How is it cooked?

What is caramel made of, and what is it used for?

What can you tell me about green vegetables; should not they be fresh?

Are they always put on in boiling water, and what kind of boiling water do you use?

Do you always put in salt?

How much?

How long a time should they generally be cooked?

Can any exact rule be given?

Why not?

How can you tell when they are done?

If tomatoes are to be served raw, how do you prepare them?

How do you peel them, and what are they dressed with?

Should not they be kept for a time in a cold place?

If tomatoes are to be cooked, how do you prepare them for peeling?

Why do you pour hot water on them?

Can you tell me some of the different ways in which tomatoes can be cooked?

After opening a can of tomatoes is it safe to leave what is not used in the can?

What should be done with it?

What are the two chief ingredients in the soup called Mock Bisque?

Why is it a convenient soup, and why is it called Mock Bisque?

What is the foundation of most sauces, and how is it made?

What is the difference between a brown roux and a white roux?

Can you make a variety of sauces from these?

What would you add if you wish to make a brown sauce, and how would you make a white sauce?

How do you prepare rice?

Must it be washed in several waters?

In making cornstarch Blanc Mange, how can you put the cornstarch into the hot milk smoothly, so that there may be no lumps?

When adding flour or any thickening to hot milk or water, do not you generally first make it into a smooth paste, and also stir them constantly?

What should be done to the moulds before the cornstarch is poured into them?

How do you mould cornstarch; in one mould, or in cups?

Can you tell me how eggs should be poached?

Can you tell me something about yeast, and what it is made of?

Where should eggs be kept?

Why should some of the egg shells be saved, when you are breaking eggs?

Why do you break each egg singly over a cup?

If an egg is fresh and good, how will the white of it look?

If you are separating the yolks from the whites, and a little of the yolk gets into the whites, how can you take it out?

How must you hold the upper arm when you are beating eggs?

What is a Dover egg-beater used for?

Why is it only good for yolks or whole eggs?

Why does it injure the whites, and what should they be beaten with?

Do you wash the upper part of a Dover egg-beater?

How do you keep the little wheels from wearing out?

Can any fixed rule be given for the amount of sugar required for a meringue?

What is a meringue made of?

Is it put on while a pudding is hot?

If you wish to brown it a little, how can you do it?

Is it safe to keep puddings or cakes which have milk, eggs, and flavorings in them?

Will they become dangerous?

Are not the juices of fresh fruit always much better than extracts?

What kind of boiler do you cook a custard in?

Must it be stirred constantly?

How can you tell when it is cooked enough, and how do you prevent it from curdling?

Do you use whole eggs, or only the yolks?
How do you serve soft custard?

ON FRYING AND THE MANAGEMENT OF FRIED DISHES.

When we immerse and cook anything in very hot fat what is it called?

What kind of kettle is used for frying?

How full of fat should it be?

How can you tell when the fat is hot enough to use?

Should not the heat of the fat in frying be as carefully regulated as an oven is for baking?

How will the lightest dough be affected if the fat is not right?

If the fat is too hot, what will happen?

If it is too cool, what effect will it have?

Do you go right on frying without stopping to let the fat heat up?

Why must you put only a few doughnuts or fishballs in at a time?

How would the chilling of the fat affect them?

Where should a kettle of hot fat always be placed?

If it were near the edge of a stove, and upset, would not the burn be much worse than that made by water?

Why must you never let any cold water touch hot fat?

Why do you put the doughnuts and fishballs into the kettle carefully with a ladle?

In making doughnuts should the dough be stiff or soft?

What shape do you make them?

When they are done, how do you take them out of the kettle?

What do you put them in for a time?

Are they ever sprinkled with powdered sugar?

Do you make them with sour milk, or sweet milk?

What is used with the sour milk, and what with the sweet milk?

When you have finished your frying, do you leave the lard in the kettle?

What do you strain it through, and what do you keep it in?

Can you add fresh lard to this?

If anything has been fried which has given the lard an unpleasant taste, how can you make it fit to use again?

How much water do you put in the kettle with the cold lard?

How can you tell when it is time to put in the potato?

How long can you continue this method of straining and renewing the lard?

Must it not occasionally be thrown away?

Is not lard better than anything else to fry doughnuts and fishballs in?

Cannot nicely prepared beef-suet be used sometimes instead of lard, for frying some things?

How do you prepare salt cod-fish for making fishballs?

Do you not find some bones even in what is called boneless cod-fish?

After it has been picked into fine strips, what do you pour over it?

Is it ever necessary to put hot water on it more than once?

How do you prepare the potatoes for fishballs?

How do you get all the water out of the fish before mixing it with the potatoes?

Why should the mixture be made as soft as possible with milk?

Why do you let the mashed potato cool?

How can you tell whether the seasoning is all right?

What shape do you make the fish-balls and what do you fry them in?

When you intend to use a frying-pan how do you prepare it?

Should it be *well* heated?

Do you heat it before or after the butter is put in?

When do you put in the butter?

Do you let it entirely melt?

If the butter is allowed to get brown how will it affect what is cooked in it?

Can you tell me how to scramble eggs?

What is considered to be the best kind of griddle?

Do you grease it?

If you have a new iron griddle which is rough, what can you do to it?

Do you heat a griddle before you are ready to cook on it?

When do you grease a griddle, and what is the best way of doing it?

If there is too much butter or lard how will it affect the cakes?

Which do you use for greasing a griddle, butter or lard?

Which do you use for bread-pans or cake pans?

Why is lard considered better for cooking over cold mush or potatoes?

In what do you keep the lard or butter, which is used for greasing pans and griddles?

When baking griddle cakes, how do you take each one out of the bowl?

Where should the bowl stand?

Do you stir the batter as you take up each cake?

Why must you clean the bottom of the spoon on the edge of the bowl as you take it out of the batter?

How much batter do you take up at a time?

Must not you use a large spoon?

Do you pour the batter in the griddle from the point or side of the spoon?

Should not the cakes be round and of uniform size?

Why should you constantly stir in the batter which collects on the side of the bowl?

What kind of bread is used for bread fritters?

What do you soak the slices in, and how do you cook them?

Can you use whole eggs for an omelet, or must you beat the whites and yolks separately?

After the mixture of eggs and milk is in the pan on the fire how do you make it of a light and porous consistency?

How do you double it onto itself in the pan?

Can you tell me what is meant by a "cutting in" motion, and how it differs from mixing and stirring?

What can you tell me about oysters?

Should they be entirely fresh?

When they are to be eaten raw, which do you select?

Can you tell me some of the different ways in which oysters can be cooked?

In preparing oysters for cooking, do you strain them?

How should you pick them over in order to remove every little piece of shell?

If oysters are cooked too long, what effect will it have on them?

How do you prepare oysters for frying, and what do you dip them into?

Do you drop them directly into the hot fat?

What else is generally fried in a wire basket?

Can you put bread crumbs back into the jar after they have been moistened?

Should invalids be allowed to eat the hard part of an oyster?

When we immerse and cook anything in a kettle of hot fat what is the process called?

When we cook anything in a saucepan or frying-pan with a small quantity of butter or lard, what is the process called?

When we are cooking cakes on a griddle what is the process called?

ON THE MANAGEMENT OF MEATS.

How should meat look when it is fresh and good?

Is not meat more tender after it has been kept for a time?

Should fresh meat ever be soaked?

How should it be cleaned?

What is the color of the best beef, and which are the best ribs for roasting?

How do you prepare these for roasting?

What is the color of the best mutton, and how do you cook a shoulder or leg of mutton?

Which are the best pieces for roasting, and which are the best for stewing?

What can you tell me about the color of the meat and fat of veal?

Which are the best pieces for roasting, and which are the best for stewing?

What kind of meat and fat should pork have?

Which is considered the most delicate piece for roasting?

Are not the leg, loin, and shoulder very good?

Should pork and veal be eaten in hot weather?

Should the oven be very hot when meat is first put into it?

Do you keep it at the same heat until the meat is done?

How many minutes to the pound do you allow for meat which is to be rare?

How many minutes should be allowed for meat which is to be well done?

Should beef and mutton be rare, or well done?

How long should veal, pork, and lamb be cooked?

How do you prepare a piece of beef which is to be roasted?

How do you put it into the meat pan?

What do you sprinkle and dredge it with while it is in the oven?

How do you prepare the butter to baste it with, and how often do you baste it?

If you are making a gravy from the drippings in the pan, what must you do first?

After every particle of fat is removed, how do you make the gravy?

If it is not thick enough, what do you add to it?

Do you ever strain it?

In what other way can gravies be made?

Are they not more wholesome?

If you have some cold beef and cabbage, how can you cook them over?

Which beefsteaks are considered the best, and how should they be cooked?

Which cuts from the round are the best for steaks?

How should the steaks from the round be cooked?

How are veal, mutton, and pork chops generally cooked?

If meat has been washed, can you cook it without drying it?

If it is not dried, will it ever brown well?

Do you ever pound tender meat?

If meat is tough, how can it be made more tender?

If you are broiling a beefsteak and are obliged to leave it for a few minutes, how can you prevent it from burning?

What kind of fire must you have for broiling?

Why do you hold each side of the steak for a moment over the fire?

What does the length of time required for broiling a steak depend on?

How many minutes does it take to cook a rare steak, and how many to cook one which is to be well done?

How do you serve a beefsteak, and how do you butter it?

Is it not better to butter it merely on the upper side?

How do you prepare meat for making hash, or minced meat?

After carefully taking out all the bone, gristle, and skin, what do you add to it?

How much cold potato do you add in proportion to the meat?

What do you cook the hash in?

Is it always necessary to use expensive materials?

Should you throw away everything that is left over?

What can cold meat bones be used for?

What can you do with the fat?

How can you use pieces of dry bread or cake?

What other things can you think of which can be cooked over?

If a little flour is wasted and thrown away every time

that you are using flour, how much will it amount to in a year?

When you are planning the breakfast and dinner what is it well to think of?

Are there not often things in the house which can be used?

What is the difference between economy and meanness?

Is not economy praiseworthy?

Can you ever warm over cold meat?

After you have cut off neatly the slices of meat, how do you cook the bone?

How long before you serve it, do you put the meat in?

What is often added to the gravy with cold beef, and what is added when cold mutton is used?

Can you use cold meat for making pies?

Can you make pies from uncooked meat?

Why is it better to have the meat at least partially cooked?

Can you cook over cold meat with any other crust?

ON THE MANAGEMENT AND COOKING OF VEGETABLES.

Can both kinds of potatoes be baked as well as boiled?

Do they require a hot oven, and how long a time should they be baked?

How can you warm over cold white potatoes for breakfast?

Cannot cold boiled sweet potatoes be sliced and cooked over for breakfast?

In boiling vegetables, how much salt should be used for a quart of water?

How do you prepare green peas, and how long do you boil them?

What is done to them after they have boiled, and how do you serve them?

How do you prepare string beans, and how long should they be cooked?

Are they drained through a colander?

How are they served, and what is added to them?

How do you prepare asparagus, and how is it cooked?

Do you cover it entirely with the boiling water?

How should it be served?

Do you peel summer squashes or cymlings?

Should the seeds be taken out?

Do you boil or steam them?

How are winter squashes prepared?

Should they be cut into large pieces?

After removing all the seeds and fibres, should not you pare the skin from these pieces?

Should not winter squash be steamed?

How long do you steam it?

After it has been mashed thoroughly, what should be added to it?

If any cold squash is left, how can it be cooked over the next day?

How do you prepare turnips, and what is the simplest way of cooking them?

After they are drained and mashed what is added to them?

Can they be cooked whole?

What kind of sauce should be served with them when they are cooked whole?

Why should a cabbage be carefully washed?

How long do you let it remain in cold water?

How do you cut it up and cook it?

When it is boiled by itself, what is added to it, and how is it served?

When it is boiled with corned beef, how is it served?

After washing parsnips and oyster plants, do you peel or scrape them?

Can you tell me some of the different ways in which they can be cooked?

Should carrots be scraped or peeled?

Are they served whole or in slices?

Should beets be washed?

Why should they never be peeled or pricked?

Are they put into boiling water?

How long should they be cooked?

After they are boiled enough, what do you lay them in for a few minutes before you rub off the skin?

How do you serve them?

If any are left over, how can you prepare them to be used the next day?

Should not winter beets be soaked over night?

Do you boil parsnips and other vegetables when you intend to make them into fritters?

Are they not sometimes fried in slices?

When they are mashed and mixed with batter, what do you fry them in?

What is a drop batter?

Cannot oysters and clams be used for making fritters?

Are they always chopped, or can they be used whole?

When apples are used for fritters cannot they be either chopped or cut in slices?

ON SALADS AND THE MANAGEMENT OF UNCOOKED VEGETABLES.

How should uncooked vegetables which are to be used for salads, be prepared and freshened?

How should they be pulled apart?

Can you tell me some of the vegetables which are generally used in salads?

With what other vegetables are sliced onions sometimes used?

When onion juice is used as a flavoring, how do you press it out?

How do you prepare and serve cucumbers?

Are not slices or small pieces of hard boiled eggs sometimes used for garnishing?

Can you tell me of anything else which is used as a garnish?

When parsley is used as a garnish, how do you break it?

When it is used in cooking, how do you prepare it?

Should not dried herbs always be rubbed through a sieve?

How can you make celery crisp?

When it is used in salads, how should it be cut?

What kinds of meats can be used for salads?

Why should they be cooked the day before they are to be used?

What kind of oil do you use in making salad dressing?

Should not most dressings be mixed quickly?

What kind of spoon or fork should be used?

Can boiled salad dressing and Mayonnaise dressing be kept for any length of time?

Where should you put them?

When you have mixed together the different ingredients which are to be used in boiled salad dressing, what do you cook them in?

Should not the dressing be constantly stirred?

When it has thickened enough, what should be done with it?

Why do you set the saucepan in a pan of cold water?

Should not cold potatoes be used for potato salad?

How do you cut them up, and how do you put them on the dish?

What do you sprinkle on each layer of potato?

Is not a little of the dressing added also?

How do you garnish them round the edge?

What do you use for garnishing the top?

Is not there a more simple dressing which can be used with lettuce and other vegetables?

Can you tell me what it is made of?

Can it be kept for a time, or should it be used at once?

Should not the best of materials be used always in making salads?

ON THE MANAGEMENT OF CAKES, DESSERTS AND PASTRY.

Can you make nice cake out of poor materials?

What should it be mixed in, and what kind of spoon do you generally use?

What is a split spoon, and which kind of cake is it used for?

What kind of knife do you use for cake which requires a "cutting in" motion

What is the best knife to use for putting the icing on cake?

Should not all the materials be ready on the table before you begin to make cake?

Ought not it be mixed lightly and made quickly?

How hot an oven does cake require?

How do you prepare the pans for cake?

Are they always buttered?

Do not some kinds of cake require a paper in the pan?

When a cake is browning too fast at the top, how can you prevent it?

How can you tell when cake is done?

Are all kinds of cake taken from the pans as soon as they are done?

Can you give me the names of some of those which are left in the pan to cool?

How do you cool the cakes which are taken out of the pan as soon as they are done?

Ought not they cool slowly?

Will not they be heavy if put suddenly in a draft of cold air?

If there is no paper used in the pan, how do you loosen the cake so that it will come out easily?

How do you cream butter?

In creaming butter and sugar together, which do you cream first?

If the batter or dough is too stiff, what should you add?

If it is not stiff enough, what should you add?

Can you tell me how the various pans which are used for cake differ from each other?

In making plain icing, which part of the egg is used?

What is added to it?

Do you make and beat icing in the same way in which you would make a meringue?

Do you flavor icing?

Are not the juices of fresh fruit much better for flavoring than even the best extracts are?

Can you tell me some of the flavorings which are most commonly used?

Can you use one flavoring in the cake, and another in the icing?

. Should lemon and extract of almond ever be used together?

When the icing is beaten to a smooth, stiff paste, how do you put it on the cake?

Should not cake be allowed to cool somewhat before the icing is put on?

Cannot some cakes be iced while they are quite warm, while others should be almost cold before the icing is put on?

If light, delicate cakes were iced while very warm, what effect would it have?

After the icing has been put on, will it harden if the cake is left in a warm place?

Is it possible to give recipes which can always be exactly followed?

Why cannot they be given?

Is flour always the same?

Is it not affected by a damp atmosphere?

Why would a difference in the size of the eggs which are used make a difference in the cake?

Are seasonings and flavorings always of the same strength?

How should you make the dough of the right consistency, if it is too stiff, even if made exactly by the recipe?

When the oven is to be used, how should the fire be prepared for it?

How long beforehand should it be cleared and have the fresh coal put on?

Should not coal enough be put on at first to last through the whole time of baking?

If it is absolutely necessary to add some, how should it be done?

Will any oven bake well directly after fresh coal has been put on the fire?

After the baking is finished, what should be done to the fire?

Should wood ever be put on top of coal?

What effect will it have?

Cannot a fire and an oven be managed so as to give no trouble?

Why is it well to make gold and silver cake at the same time?

If both are to be used at once, in what kind of pans is it well to bake them?

Should not the batter for the silver cake be made rather stiff?

Is it well to beat the whites of the eggs very stiff for silver cake?

If eggs are beaten too long or too stiff, will not it cause a little dryness in the consistency of cake?

In rolling and cutting ginger-snaps, why must you cut all that you can from each rolling of the dough?

What should their color be when they are baked?

What should bread be kept in, and what should cake be kept in?

Can you shut them up tight in a box while they are warm?

If bread and cake are cooled too rapidly, how will it affect them?

What should the pieces of clean bread be kept in?

What can they be used for?

How do you prepare bread crumbs?
What should they be kept in, and what are they used for?
Why should the tin moulds for desserts be kept very bright and clean?
What should be done to a pudding cloth before the pudding is put into it?
Why should the cloth be left a little loose?
Is the string left loose also?
Why should the string be tied very tight?
Should the water be kept boiling until the pudding is done?
Should not puddings be cooked as soon as they are mixed?
Why does it particularly hurt them to stand when there is dried fruit in them?
How should dried currants be prepared?
Should not raisins always be seeded before they are used for cake or desserts?
What do you dredge dried fruits with?
How can you take Blanc Mange, jellies and ice-cream easily from the moulds?
What can be added to a bread pudding if you wish to make it richer than you usually make it?
How do you make cold sauce for puddings?
How do you prepare the butter and sugar for hot sauce?
After beating them together, what do you pour onto them?
What flavorings are generally used in hot sauces?
Should not the materials which are used in cooking always be of the best quality?
When you are stirring batter or anything else in a bowl, why is it important to mix in constantly all of it which remains on the side of the bowl?

If this is not done, will not the batter be unequally mixed, and often have little lumps in it?

If batter is poured from one bowl to another what should you be careful to do?

Should a metal spoon be used for measuring acids?

Should it be used for mixing anything which has acid in it?

Is it well to leave a spoon standing in anything which you are mixing or cooking?

On what should you lay the spoon?

How can you tell whether a dish is properly seasoned or flavored?

In what way can you taste it neatly and nicely?

What is better than a spoon for beating up a thin batter?

Should batter be left standing after it is mixed?

Can the yolks or whites of eggs be kept good for a day or two, if there are any left unused?

Will the oven bake well if there is a cover off of the stove?

If the meat for dinner is to be broiled over the fire, what kind of desserts is it best to have?

How do you scald cornmeal?

What is the difference between custard and custard sauce?

How can you make a nice dessert out of a dry sponge cake?

How should rice be prepared for use?

Is it used only as a vegetable?

What desserts or breakfast dishes can be made from it?

If you are cooking over cold rice, how do you soften it?

Would not the puddings or cakes otherwise be full of lumps?

What are sago and tapioca used for, and how must they be prepared?

How many kinds of tapioca are there?
When should tapioca be put in soak?
How long should sago be soaked?
If tapioca is to be cooked for a late dinner, cannot it be put in soak in the morning?
Cannot very nice baked puddings be made from rice, tapioca or sago?
How do you prepare the apples for an apple and tapioca pudding?
How should sweet apples be cooked?
Why are sour apples always used for puddings, pies, and sauces?
Can you mention the names of the apples which are generally used for cooking?
Which do you use for making apple pies?
What is paste made of?
Is not butter more wholesome than lard?
Which will make the paste tender, and which will make it flaky?
How can you freshen butter which is too salt?
Should not paste be made quickly and in a cold place?
Should more flour be added if the dough becomes soft from being worked?
If flour is constantly added, will not the paste be tough and heavy?
How can you make the dough stiff and hard without using flour?
If you are using both butter and lard, which is worked into the flour first?
How do you rub butter or lard into flour?
After the dough is mixed how do you roll it?
Should the dough for the under paste be stretched tightly over the pie plate?

Why should it be lifted once or twice in laying it on?

Why should the upper crust always be pricked with a fork?

How can you prevent the juice from running out of a pie?

How does rich-paste differ from plain paste?

Cannot this same paste be used also for meat pies?

ON THE MANAGEMENT AND COOKING OF BREAKFAST DISHES.

Should not coffee, tea, cocoa, and chocolate be made just before they are to be served?

If they are boiled or steeped too long, how will it affect them?

Should not the water which is used for making tea and coffee be actually boiling?

Should water which has been boiling for an hour or two be used for tea or coffee?

Why is it unfit for use?

Why is it very important that coffee-pots and tea-pots should be kept thoroughly clean?

Should tea be made in a tin tea-pot?

If a silver tea-pot is used, should it ever be put on or near the stove?

What should coffee and tea be kept in?

Why should coffee which is already roasted be bought in small quantities?

Can you tell me how to roast coffee in an oven?

How hot should the oven be?

What do you stir it with?

MANUAL OF COOKERY.

Can you make good coffee from coffee beans which have been unequally roasted?

If they are burnt, how will the coffee taste?

Is not it better to use always freshly ground coffee?

Can you tell me the names of some of the different kinds of coffee?

In what proportion are Java and Mocha coffees sometimes mixed?

Is not the coffee very nice which is made from this mixture?

How much coffee and how much egg shell is allowed for every cupful of water?

After the coffee-pot is scalded, what do you put into it first?

How much cold water is put in with the coffee?

What do you add next?

After pouring on the boiling water, how long should the coffee boil?

How do you clear the grounds from the spout of the coffee-pot?

How can you make stronger coffee if it is desired?

Can you tell me how drip coffee is made?

After scalding the tea-pot how much tea do you put in?

Do you pour on all the boiling water at once?

How is English breakfast tea made?

Is it well to drink very strong tea or coffee, or to drink them too often?

How many kinds of cornmeal are there?

Will you tell me some of the dishes which can be made with cornmeal?

When sugar, salt, soda, or any other powders are used in cooking, how do you free them from lumps?

How much cream of tartar is used with one teaspoonful of soda?

How much flour is used with this quantity of soda and cream of tartar?

If soda is used with sour milk, how much of it is required, and how do you dissolve it?

If it is not used with sour milk, how do you dissolve it?

Why is it better to dissolve it?

How much baking powder is required for a pint of flour?

Why are the salt and the baking powder generally sifted in with the flour?

When soda or baking powder are used, should not the batter be quickly mixed and baked?

Will not batter become heavy if it is not cooked as soon as it is mixed?

In putting ingredients together how should the flour and milk be added?

If they were put in carelessly and quickly, what effect would it have?

If a small quantity of flour is used for thickening sauces or gravies, or anything else, what should it be mixed with before it is put in?

When used for gravies is it better to mix it with water or with melted butter?

If butter is melted over too hot a fire, or is kept too long on the stove, how will it affect it?

How should it be melted?

How can butter be softened a little without melting it?

Can you tell me how oatmeal should be cooked?

How long should steamed oatmeal be boiled?

What should oatmeal be boiled in?

What is graham meal used for?

Is not it much better to use the various kinds of meal sometimes in our food, instead of using nothing but white flour?

Why should tepid water or milk be used always with yeast?

How would hot water or milk affect it?

Can you tell me how eggs should be boiled?

How long a time is required to cook eggs which are to be very soft?

How many minutes will it take to cook them if the whites are to be firmly set?

How long are hard-boiled eggs generally boiled?

Will not they be more wholesome if they are cooked half an hour?

Can you tell me some of the breakfast dishes which can be made from bread which has become a little dry?

How do you prepare the bread for making bread griddle cakes?

What are waffles baked in?

Why is it important that the waffle-iron should be perfectly clean?

How do you prepare the waffle-iron for baking waffles?

How much batter should be put in at a time?

After putting in the batter, why is it best to wait until it has had time to stiffen a little, before turning the waffle-iron?

If it were turned while the batter is soft, would not this fall and become heavy?

If waffles and Sally Lunns are to be used at supper, what should they be sprinkled with?

How can the recipe for Sally Lunns be changed and used for making breakfast muffins?

Can you tell me what short cake is made of?

How do you roll and bake it when it is to be used for breakfast?

How do you bake it when it is to be used for a strawberry or fruit short cake?

When you are kneading dough on a board, why should the little pieces be constantly gathered in?

Can you tell me how cornmeal mush should be made?

If there is any left over how can you cook it for breakfast the next day?

If too much butter and milk are used in cooking, what effect will it have?

If you wish to succeed in cooking, what must you pay attention to?

ON THE MANAGEMENT AND COOKING OF FISH, POULTRY, AND SALT MEATS.

Why should fish be selected with great care?

How can you tell whether a fish is fresh?

How do you prepare them before they are cooked, and where should they be kept?

Can you tell me some of the different ways in which fish may be cooked?

How are large and medium sized fish generally cooked?

How are small fish generally cooked?

If any cold fish is left over, how can you cook it nicely for breakfast the next day?

Can you tell me how to boil a fish?

Why should it be wrapped in a cloth?

Can you tell me which slice of a salmon is the best piece to boil?

What part of a cod is the best piece to boil?

In serving boiled fish what must you be very careful to do?

What kind of sauce is generally served with boiled fish?

Can you tell me how to cook a small fish in a frying pan?

How should a large fish be fried?

How do you prepare a fish for broiling?

Which side should be held first to the fire?

Should not fish which are to be fried or broiled, be thoroughly dried after they have been washed?

Why do large fish require a more moderate fire than small ones?

How should poultry look when they are healthy and good?

How should they be killed?

How long a time should they be kept before they are cooked?

If you are buying those which have been killed, how can you tell whether they are tender and fresh?

If a turkey or chicken is to be boned, why should you select one which has not been scalded?

After the feathers are pulled out, how do you remove the pin feathers?

Can you tell me how a turkey or chicken should be cleaned and prepared for cooking?

What should be done with the liver, neck, heart and gizzard?

What are these used for?

After the liver has been boiled how do you prepare it for making the gravy?

How should the gizzard be served?

Should hams, tongues and corned beef be put on in hot or cold water?

Why should they always be boiled slowly and gently?

What effect would hard boiling have on them?

If corned beef is to be served cold, how do you press it?

Should not a ham be put in soak overnight?

After it has been boiled enough and has partly cooled, what should be done to it?

What can a cold ham bone be used for?

What should be trimmed off of slices of ham which are to be fried or broiled?

How can you prepare a nice dish for luncheon or breakfast from what is left of a cold ham, or from the roots of a tongue?

ON THE PREPARATION OF BEEF-TEA AND A FEW DISHES FOR THE SICK.

Why cannot any fixed rules be given in regard to food and diet?

What general rule can be given however in regard to the relation between well cooked food and good health?

Is not cooking a distinct art by itself?

What kind of food should be given to persons who are sick?

How do you prepare beef-essence and how strong is it?

What is the largest quantity of it which should be given at a time?

What effect will a half teaspoonful of it given every hour sometimes have on a very sick person?

How is the beef prepared for making beef-tea?

What should be used for cutting it up?

Why should not it be chopped in a tray?

Can you tell me a good rule for giving beef-tea?

Why is it important to give sick persons some nourishment in the night?

In making milk porridge how can you add the flour to the milk smoothly and without lumps?

Can you tell me some of the different kinds of gruel which may be given to those who are sick?

Are there not many delicate dishes which can be prepared for them and for convalescents?

While it is very important that they should be kept well nourished, should we not be careful also not to give them too much?

ON COOKING UTENSILS AND THE CLEANING AND WASHING OF DISHES.

What should the motto be for every kitchen and pantry?

Should not all dishes and cooking utensils be kept thoroughly clean and bright?

What should such materials as flour, rice, and sugar be kept in?

Should cornstarch, oatmeal and other materials which come in packages be left in the paper?

What should salt be kept in, and why should it never be kept in anything which is made of tin?

Should not every box and jar be properly labelled?

Will not this save time and trouble, and also prevent perhaps some dangerous mistake?

Why should there be a tin match box in every kitchen?

Why should a refrigerator be kept clean and well aired?

Should anything hot or even warm ever be put into a refrigerator?

How will fruit and vegetables affect butter and milk, if they are kept near each other or shut up together?

How should bread and cake boxes be aired?

How do acids act on tin, zinc, and some kinds of glazed earthen ware?

Why are copper utensils dangerous unless they are kept perfectly clean?

Are not bowls better than tin pans for mixing purposes?

Why is it convenient to have a piece of zinc on the table?

What kind of bowls should be kept purposely for milk?

How many different kinds of towels should there be in a kitchen?

What other cloths are needed beside dish cloths?

Can you tell me the names of some of the cooking utensils which are required in every kitchen?

How many dredging boxes should there be, and what are they used for?

Should they be of the same color?

Can you tell me some of the different kinds of knives and spoons which are required?

Why should there be one or two coffee cups in a kitchen?

How much does a coffee cup hold?

Can you recite the tables in the twelfth lesson?

If iron kettles or pans have been neglected, what can you clean them with?

What do you use for cleaning tin and wooden ware?

How should wood always be rubbed?

How do you clean a bread board?

Why is it well to put a little tepid water into kettles and

saucepans as soon as you have taken out what has been cooked in them?

Why is it well to keep an old pan or dish near the sink?

Is not it easier to put any little garbage there may be into that, and carry it all out at once than it is to keep running out to the garbage bucket?

Should not both of them be kept very clean?

Does not garbage become unwholesome if it is allowed to stand long?

Where do you wash the iron and tin kettles and pans?

Where should the nicer dishes be washed?

Should not they first be gathered neatly together and scraped?

Can you wash dishes clean in cold or greasy water?

Should not it always be hot and clean?

How many waters do you wash them in?

Why should each dish be stood separately after it is wiped?

Should not the knives and forks and spoons be laid separately also after they are wiped?

Can you wipe dishes nicely with damp towels?

If you are washing nice parlor dishes, which should be washed first?

Why should the silver and glass be washed first?

Which dishes should be washed next?

Why should the cups and saucers be washed before the plates?

If there are glasses which have been used for eggs, why do you put cold water into them, and let them stand for a time before washing them?

If a glass dish or tumbler is dipped into hot water in such a way that both the inside and outside are wet at the same time, will not it prevent the heat from cracking it?

NOTES FOR THE TEACHER.

The directions for cleaning and washing dishes were not given in the lessons, because the teacher is expected to show the pupils how to do this, and also to watch them and see that everything is properly washed and dried, and put into its right place after each lesson. One girl should be selected to clear off the table, another one to wash the dishes, and another to wipe them and put them away.

The teacher will find that there are only thirty-three lessons instead of thirty-four, as a mistake occured in the numbering of them which was not discovered until it was too late to correct it. The lessons are all in the right order, and if they are dictated, it will be easy to correct it. In the recipe for mock apple pie the quantity of sugar which should be used (two-thirds of a cupful) was unintentionally omitted. As tablespoonful, teaspoonful, and some other words are generally abbreviated now, it may be well to say that I have preferred to use the whole word, because the abbreviations so nearly resemble each other, that a serious mistake might easily occur, and also because it requires quite an effort of thought to understand the abbreviations, which the child might as well be spared.

LIBRARY OF CONGRESS

0 014 485 856 6

www.ingramcontent.com/pod-product-compliance
Lightning Source LLC
Chambersburg PA
CBHW031335160426
43196CB00007B/701